RIVAL Crock Pot ®

The Original and #1 Brand Slow Cooker

Simple 1-2-3
Slow Cooker
RECIPES

pil

Publications International, Ltd.

Louis Weber, CEO
Publications International, Ltd.
7373 North Cicero Avenue
Lincolnwood, IL 60712

Pictured on front cover: Slow Cooker Cassoulet *(page 63)*.

Pictured on back cover: Burgundy Beef Po' Boys with Dipping Sauce *(page 34),* Warm Blue Crab Bruschetta *(page 18),* and Chili Verde *(page 94).*

Photography on pages 18, 19, 26, 27, 28, 34, 41, 42, 43, 47, 48, 49, 50, 51, 52, 53, 63, 64, 65, 66, 67, 78, 88, 89, 90, 91, 94, 103, 120 ,122, 123, 124, 133, 134, 135, 144, 147, 149, 150, 151, 152 and 153 by Stephen Hamilton Photographics, Chicago.

Photographers: Tate Hunt, Eric Coughlin
Photographers' Assistant: Christy Clow
Prop Stylist: Tom Hamilton
Food Stylists: Kim Hartman, Rick Longhi, Mary Helen Steindler
Assistant Food Stylists: Constance Pikulas, Christina Zerkis

ISBN 13: 978-1-4127-2496-8
ISBN 10: 1-4127-2496-1

Manufactured in China.

8 7 6 5 4 3 2 1

Contents

Slow Cooking Basics

This fast guide to slow cooking will enhance your experience and your results. You'll wonder how you ever got along without your Crock-Pot® slow cooker.

Stirring

Due to the nature of a slow cooker, there's no need to stir the food unless it specifically says to in your recipe. In fact, taking the lid off to stir food causes the slow cooker to lose a significant amount of heat, extending the cooking time required. Therefore, it's best not to remove the lid for stirring.

Cooking Temperatures and Food Safety

Cooking meats in your **CROCK-POT**® slow cooker is perfectly safe. According to the U.S. Department of Agriculture, bacteria in food are killed at a temperature of 165°F. Meats cooked in the **CROCK-POT**® slow cooker reach an internal temperature in excess of 170°F for beef and as high as 209°F for poultry. It's important to follow the recommended cooking times and to keep the cover on your **CROCK-POT**® slow cooker during the cooking process.

If your food isn't done after 8 hours when the recipe calls for 8 to 10 hours, this could be due to voltage variations, which are commonplace; to altitude; or even to extreme humidity. Slight fluctuations in power don't have a noticeable effect on most appliances; however, they can slightly alter the cooking times. Allow plenty of time, and remember:

It's practically impossible to overcook in a **CROCK-POT**® slow cooker. You'll learn through experience whether to decrease or increase cooking times.

Removable Stoneware

The removable stoneware in your **CROCK-POT**® slow cooker makes cleaning easy. Here are some tips on the use and care of your stoneware:

- Don't preheat your **CROCK-POT**® slow cooker.

- Your **CROCK-POT**® slow cooker makes a great server for dips, appetizers or hot beverages. Keep it on the WARM setting to maintain the proper serving temperature.

- Because all **CROCK-POT**® slow cookers have wrap-around heat, there is no direct heat from the bottom. For best results, always fill the stoneware at least half full to conform to recommended times. Small quantities can still be cooked, but cooking times will be affected.

Browning Meat

Meat cooked in the **CROCK-POT**® slow cooker will not brown as it would if it were cooked in a skillet or oven at high temperatures. For some recipes, it's not necessary to brown meat before slow cooking. If you prefer the flavor and look of browned meat, however, simply brown the meat in a large skillet coated with nonstick cooking spray before placing it in the stoneware and following the recipe as written.

Adding Ingredients at the End of the Cooking Time

Certain ingredients tend to break down during extended cooking. When possible, add these ingredients toward the end of the cooking time:

- Milk, cream, and sour cream: Add during the last 15 minutes of cooking time.

- Seafood: Add in the last 3 to 15 minutes, depending on the thickness and quantity. Gently stir periodically to ensure even cooking.

Cooking for Larger Quantity Yields

Follow these guidelines when preparing recipes in a larger unit, such as a 5-, 6-, or 7-quart **CROCK-POT**® slow cooker:

- Roasted meats, chicken, and turkey quantities may be doubled or tripled, but seasonings should be adjusted by no more than half. Flavorful seasonings, such as garlic and chili powder, intensify during long, slow cooking. Add just 25 to 50 percent more spices, or as needed to balance flavors.

- When preparing a soup or a stew, you may double all ingredients except seasonings (see above), dried herbs, liquids, and thickeners. Increase liquid volume by no more than half, or as needed. The **CROCK-POT**® slow cooker lid collects steam, which condenses to keep foods moist and to maintain liquid volume. Don't double thickeners, such as cornstarch, at the beginning. You may always add more thickener later, if needed.

- When preparing dishes with beef or pork in a larger unit, such as a 5-, 6-, or 7-quart **CROCK-POT**® slow cooker, browning the meat in a skillet before adding it to the stoneware yields the best results; the meat will cook more evenly.

- When preparing baked goods, it is best not to double or triple the recipe. Simply prepare the original recipe as many times as needed to serve more people.

Spectacular Starts

Chai Tea

2 quarts (8 cups) water
8 bags black tea
¾ cup sugar*
16 whole cloves
16 whole cardamom seeds, pods removed (optional)
5 cinnamon sticks
8 slices fresh ginger
1 cup milk

Chai tea is typically a sweet drink. For tea that is less sweet, reduce sugar to ½ cup.

1. Combine water, tea, sugar, cloves, cardamom, if desired, cinnamon and ginger in **CROCK-POT®** slow cooker. Cover; cook on HIGH 2 to 2½ hours.

2. Strain mixture; discard solids. (At this point, tea may be covered and refrigerated up to 3 days).

3. Stir in milk just before serving. Serve warm or chilled.

Makes 8 to 10 servings

Triple Delicious Hot Chocolate

⅓ cup sugar
¼ cup unsweetened cocoa powder
¼ teaspoon salt
3 cups milk, divided
¾ teaspoon vanilla
1 cup heavy cream
1 square (1 ounce) bittersweet chocolate
1 square (1 ounce) white chocolate
¾ cup whipped cream
6 teaspoons mini chocolate chips or shaved bittersweet chocolate

1. Combine sugar, cocoa, salt and ½ cup milk in medium bowl. Beat until smooth. Pour into **CROCK-POT**® slow cooker. Add remaining 2½ cups milk and vanilla; stir in. Cover; cook on LOW 2 hours.

2. Add cream. Cover; cook on LOW 10 minutes. Stir in bittersweet and white chocolates until melted.

3. Pour hot chocolate into 6 coffee cups. Top each with 2 tablespoons whipped cream and 1 teaspoon chocolate chips.

Makes 6 servings

Asian-Spiced Chicken Wings

1. Preheat broiler. Place chicken wings on broiler pan. Broil 10 minutes on each side, or until chicken wings are brown. Transfer to **CROCK-POT**® slow cooker.

2. Add sugar, soy sauce, ketchup, ginger, garlic and sherry; stir thoroughly. Cover; cook on LOW 5 to 6 hours or on HIGH 2 to 3 hours or until chicken wings are no longer pink, stirring once halfway through cooking time to baste wings with sauce.

3. Remove wings from **CROCK-POT**® slow cooker. Reserve ¼ cup of cooking liquid; combine with hoisin sauce and lime juice. Drizzle mixture over chicken wings. Sprinkle on sesame seeds and green onions before serving.

Makes 10 to 16 wings

Tip: For 5-, 6- or 7-quart **CROCK-POT**® slow cooker, increase chicken wings to 5 pounds.

3 pounds chicken wings
1 cup packed brown sugar
1 cup soy sauce
½ cup ketchup
2 teaspoons fresh ginger, minced
2 cloves garlic, minced
¼ cup dry sherry
½ cup hoisin sauce
1 tablespoon fresh lime juice
3 tablespoons sesame seeds, toasted
¼ cup green onions, thinly sliced

2 tea bags
1 cup boiling water
1 bottle (48 ounces)
    cranberry juice
½ cup dried cranberries
    (optional)
⅓ cup sugar
1 large lemon, cut into
    ¼-inch slices
4 cinnamon sticks
6 whole cloves
  Additional thin lemon
    slices and cinnamon
    sticks for garnish

Mulled Cranberry Tea

1. Place tea bags in **CROCK-POT**® slow cooker. Pour boiling water over tea bags; cover and let stand 5 minutes. Remove and discard tea bags.

2. Stir in cranberry juice, cranberries, if desired, sugar, lemon slices, 4 cinnamon sticks and cloves. Cover; cook on LOW 2 to 3 hours or on HIGH 1 to 2 hours.

3. Remove and discard cooked lemon slices, cinnamon sticks and cloves. Serve in warm mug with fresh lemon slice and cinnamon stick.

Makes 8 servings

Slow Cooker Cheese Dip

1. Brown ground beef and sausage in medium skillet over medium-high heat, stirring to break up meat. Drain and discard fat. Transfer to **CROCK-POT®** slow cooker.

2. Add processed cheese, jalapeño peppers, onion, Cheddar cheese, cream cheese, cottage cheese, sour cream, tomatoes and garlic to **CROCK-POT®** slow cooker. Season with salt and pepper.

3. Cover; cook on HIGH 1½ to 2 hours or until cheeses are melted. Serve with crackers or tortilla chips.

Makes 16 to 18 servings

1 pound ground beef
1 pound bulk Italian sausage
1 package (16 ounces) pasteurized processed cheese spread, cubed
1 can (11 ounces) sliced jalapeño peppers, drained
1 medium onion, diced
8 ounces Cheddar cheese, cubed
1 package (8 ounces) cream cheese, cubed
1 container (8 ounces) cottage cheese
1 container (8 ounces) sour cream
1 can (8 ounces) diced tomatoes, drained
3 cloves garlic, minced
Salt and pepper, to taste

Spectacular Starts

32 pieces chicken wing
      drums and flats
 1 cup chopped red onion
 1 cup soy sauce
 ¾ cup packed light brown
      sugar
 ¼ cup dry cooking sherry
 2 tablespoons chopped
      fresh ginger
 2 cloves garlic, minced
      Chopped fresh chives

Oriental Chicken Wings

1. Preheat broiler. Broil chicken wings about 5 minutes per side. Transfer chicken to **CROCK-POT**® slow cooker.

2. Combine onion, soy sauce, sugar, sherry, ginger and garlic in large bowl. Add to **CROCK-POT**® slow cooker; stir to blend well. Cover; cook on LOW 5 to 6 hours or on HIGH 2 to 3 hours.

3. Sprinkle with chives before serving.

Makes 32 appetizers

Spectacular Starts

Cocktail Meatballs

1. Preheat oven to 350°F. Combine beef, sausage, cracker crumbs, onion, bell pepper, milk, egg, salt, Italian seasoning and pepper in bowl. Mix well; form into 1-inch meatballs. Place meatballs onto 2 nonstick baking sheets. Bake 25 minutes or until browned.

2. Meanwhile, place ketchup, sugar, butter, vinegar, lemon juice, water, mustard and garlic salt into **CROCK-POT**® slow cooker; mix well. Cover; cook on HIGH until hot.

3. Transfer meatballs to **CROCK-POT**® slow cooker; carefully stir to coat with sauce. Reduce heat to LOW. Cover; cook 2 hours.

Makes 12 servings

1 pound ground beef
1 pound bulk pork or Italian sausage
1 cup cracker crumbs
1 cup finely chopped onion
1 cup finely chopped green bell pepper
½ cup milk
1 egg, beaten
2 teaspoons salt
1 teaspoon dried Italian seasoning
¼ teaspoon black pepper
1 cup ketchup
¾ cup packed brown sugar
½ cup (1 stick) butter
½ cup vinegar
¼ cup lemon juice
¼ cup water
1 teaspoon mustard
¼ teaspoon garlic salt

Mocha Supreme

2 quarts strong brewed coffee
½ cup instant hot chocolate beverage mix
1 cinnamon stick, broken into halves
1 cup whipping cream
1 tablespoon powdered sugar

1. Place coffee, hot chocolate mix and cinnamon stick halves in **CROCK-POT®** slow cooker; stir. Cover; cook on HIGH 2 to 2½ hours or until hot.

2. Remove and discard cinnamon stick halves.

3. Beat cream in medium bowl with electric mixer on high speed until soft peaks form. Add powdered sugar; beat until stiff peaks form. Ladle hot beverage into mugs; top with whipped cream.

Makes 8 servings

Tip: To whip cream more quickly, chill the beaters and bowl in the freezer for 15 minutes.

Spectacular Starts

Honey-Sauced Chicken Wings

1. Preheat broiler. Cut off and discard chicken wing tips. Cut each wing at joint to make two sections. Sprinkle wing parts with salt and pepper. Place on broiler pan. Broil 4 to 5 inches from heat 20 minutes or until chicken wings are brown, turning once. Transfer to **CROCK-POT**® slow cooker.

2. For sauce, combine honey, soy sauce, onion, ketchup, oil, garlic and pepper flakes in bowl. Pour over chicken wings.

3. Cover; cook on LOW 4 to 5 hours or on HIGH 2 to 2½ hours. Garnish with sesame seeds, if desired.

Makes about 32 appetizers

3 pounds chicken wings
1 teaspoon salt
½ teaspoon black pepper
1 cup honey
½ cup soy sauce
¼ cup chopped onion
¼ cup ketchup
2 tablespoons vegetable oil
2 cloves garlic, minced
¼ teaspoon red pepper flakes
Toasted sesame seeds (optional)

Warm Blue Crab Bruschetta

4 cups peeled, seeded and diced Roma tomatoes
1 cup diced white onion
2 teaspoons minced garlic
⅓ cup olive oil
2 tablespoons balsamic vinegar
½ teaspoon dried oregano
2 tablespoons sugar
1 pound lump blue crabmeat, picked over
1½ teaspoons kosher salt
½ teaspoon cracked black pepper
⅓ cup minced fresh basil
2 baguettes, sliced and toasted

1. Combine tomatoes, onion, garlic, oil, vinegar, oregano and sugar in **CROCK-POT**® slow cooker. Cover; cook on LOW 2 hours.

2. Add crabmeat, salt and pepper. Stir gently to mix, taking care not to break up crabmeat lumps. Cook on LOW 1 hour.

3. Fold in basil leaves. Serve on toasted baguette slices.

Makes 16 servings

Tip: Crab appetizer also can be served with Melba toast or whole-grain crackers.

Warm and Spicy Fruit Punch

1. Break cinnamon into pieces. Using vegetable peeler, remove strips of orange peel. Squeeze juice from orange; set aside.

2. Rinse cheesecloth; squeeze out water. Wrap cinnamon, orange peel, allspice, and cloves in cheesecloth. Tie bag securely with cotton string or strip of cheesecloth.

3. Combine reserved orange juice, water, concentrates and apricot nectar in **CROCK-POT**® slow cooker; add spice bag. Cover; cook on LOW 5 to 6 hours. Remove and discard spice bag before serving.

Makes about 14 (6-ounce) servings

4 cinnamon sticks
1 orange
1 teaspoon whole allspice
½ teaspoon whole cloves
1 square (8 inches) double-thickness cheesecloth
7 cups water
1 can (12 ounces) frozen cranberry-raspberry juice concentrate, thawed
1 can (6 ounces) frozen lemonade concentrate, thawed
2 cans (5½ ounces each) apricot nectar

Best-Loved Beef

Barley Beef Stroganoff

⅔ cup uncooked pearl
    barley (not
    quick-cooking)
2½ cups fat-free,
    low-sodium vegetable
    broth or water
1 package (6 ounces)
    sliced fresh
    mushrooms
½ teaspoon dried
    marjoram
½ pound 95% lean ground
    beef
½ cup chopped celery
½ cup minced green onion
½ teaspoon black pepper
¼ cup fat-free
    half-and-half
Minced fresh parsley
    (optional)

1. Place barley, broth, mushrooms and marjoram in **CROCK-POT®** slow cooker. Cover; cook on LOW 6 to 7 hours.

2. Cook and stir ground beef in large nonstick skillet over medium heat until browned and crumbly, about 7 minutes. Drain fat and discard. Add celery, green onion and pepper; cook and stir 3 minutes. Transfer to **CROCK-POT®** slow cooker.

3. Stir in half-and-half. Cover; cook on HIGH 10 to 15 minutes, until beef is hot and vegetables are tender. Garnish with minced fresh parsley, if desired.

Makes 4 servings

Beef with Apples and Sweet Potatoes

1 boneless beef chuck
  shoulder roast
  (2 pounds)
1 can (40 ounces) sweet
  potatoes, drained
2 small onions, sliced
2 apples, cored and sliced
½ cup beef broth
2 cloves garlic, minced
1 teaspoon salt
1 teaspoon dried thyme,
  divided
¾ teaspoon black pepper,
  divided
1 tablespoon cornstarch
¼ teaspoon ground
  cinnamon
2 tablespoons cold water

1. Trim excess fat from beef and discard. Cut beef into 2-inch pieces. Place beef, sweet potatoes, onions, apples, broth, garlic, salt, ½ teaspoon thyme and ½ teaspoon pepper in **CROCK-POT**® slow cooker. Cover; cook on LOW 8 to 9 hours.

2. Transfer beef, sweet potatoes and apples to platter; cover with foil to keep warm. Let cooking liquid stand 5 minutes to allow fat to rise. Skim off fat and discard.

3. Stir together cornstarch, remaining ½ teaspoon thyme, remaining ¼ teaspoon pepper, cinnamon and water until smooth; stir into cooking liquid. Cook 15 minutes on HIGH or until cooking liquid is thickened. Serve sauce with beef, sweet potatoes and apples.

Makes 6 servings

Sloppy Sloppy Joes

1. Brown beef in large skillet over medium-high heat, stirring to break up meat. Drain fat and discard.

2. Add onion and bell pepper; cook 5 to 10 minutes, stirring frequently, or until onion is translucent and mixture is fragrant.

3. Transfer meat mixture to **CROCK-POT**® slow cooker. Add remaining ingredients, except buns; stir until well blended. Cover; cook on LOW 4 to 6 hours. Serve on buns.

Makes 20 to 25 servings

4 pounds ground beef
1 cup chopped onion
1 cup chopped green bell pepper
1 can (about 28 ounces) tomato sauce
2 cans (10¾ ounces each) condensed tomato soup, undiluted
1 cup packed brown sugar
¼ cup ketchup
3 tablespoons Worcestershire sauce
1 tablespoon dry mustard
1 tablespoon prepared mustard
1½ teaspoons chili powder
1 teaspoon garlic powder
Toasted hamburger buns

Spanish-Style Couscous

1 pound lean ground beef
1 can (about 14 ounces) beef broth
1 small green bell pepper, cut into ½-inch pieces
½ cup pimiento-stuffed green olives, sliced
½ medium onion, chopped
2 cloves garlic, minced
1 teaspoon ground cumin
½ teaspoon dried thyme
1⅓ cups water
1 cup uncooked couscous

1. Brown beef in large skillet over medium-high heat, stirring to break up meat. Drain fat and discard.

2. Place broth, bell pepper, olives, onion, garlic, cumin, thyme and beef in **CROCK-POT®** slow cooker. Cover; cook on LOW 4 hours or until bell pepper is tender.

3. Bring water to a boil over high heat in small saucepan. Stir in couscous. Cover; remove from heat. Let stand 5 minutes; fluff with fork. Spoon couscous onto plates; top with beef mixture.

Makes 4 servings

Portugese Madeira Beef Shanks

1. Place garlic, onion, bell pepper, jalapeño peppers, celery and parsley in **CROCK-POT**® slow cooker.

2. Rub beef shanks with rosemary and salt. Place shanks on top of vegetables. Pour broth and wine over shanks and vegetables. Cover; cook on LOW 7 to 9 hours.

3. To serve, spoon 1 cup rice into each soup plate. Top rice with beef shank. Spoon vegetable sauce over shanks. Offer horseradish sauce, if desired.

Makes 4 servings

4 cloves garlic, minced
1 large white onion, diced
1 green bell pepper, cored and diced
2 jalapeño peppers, seeded and minced
½ cup diced celery
½ cup minced parsley
4 medium beef shanks, bone in (about 3 pounds total)
1 tablespoon fresh rosemary, minced
1 teaspoon salt, or to taste
1 cup beef broth
1 cup dry Madeira wine
4 cups hot steamed rice
   Horseradish sauce (optional)

Classic Spaghetti

2 tablespoons olive oil
2 onions, chopped
4 teaspoons minced garlic
2 green bell peppers,
    sliced
2 stalks celery, sliced
3 pounds ground beef
2 carrots, diced
1 cup mushrooms, sliced
1 can (28 ounces) tomato
    sauce
3 cups water
1 can (28 ounces) stewed
    tomatoes, undrained
1 tablespoon dried
    oregano
2 tablespoons minced
    parsley
2 teaspoons salt
2 teaspoons black pepper
1 tablespoon sugar
1 pound dry spaghetti

1. Heat oil in large skillet over medium-high heat until hot. Add onion, garlic, bell pepper and celery; cook and stir until tender. Place mixture in **CROCK-POT**® slow cooker. In same skillet, brown ground beef. Drain and discard fat; add beef to **CROCK-POT**® slow cooker.

2. Add carrots, mushrooms, tomato sauce, water, tomatoes with juice, oregano, parsley, salt, pepper and sugar to **CROCK-POT**® slow cooker. Cover; cook on LOW 6 to 8 hours or on HIGH 3 to 5 hours.

3. Cook spaghetti according to package directions; drain. Serve sauce over cooked spaghetti.

Makes 6 to 8 servings

Philly Cheese Steaks

1. Combine steak, butter, onions, bell pepper, garlic-pepper blend and salt in **CROCK-POT®** slow cooker; stir to mix.

2. Whisk together water and bouillon in small bowl; pour into **CROCK-POT®** slow cooker. Cover; cook on LOW 6 to 8 hours.

3. Remove meat, onions and bell pepper from **CROCK-POT®** slow cooker and pile on rolls. Top beef with cheese and place under broiler until cheese is melted.

Makes 8 servings

2 pounds round steak, sliced
2 tablespoons butter or margarine, melted
4 onions, sliced
2 green bell peppers, sliced
1 tablespoon garlic-pepper blend
Salt, to taste
½ cup water
2 teaspoons beef bouillon granules
8 crusty Italian or French rolls*, sliced in half
8 slices Cheddar cheese, cut in half

Toast buns on griddle or under broiler, if desired.

Hot Beef Sandwiches Au Jus

4 pounds beef rump roast
2 envelopes (1 ounce
 each) dried onion
 soup mix
2 teaspoons sugar
1 teaspoon dried oregano
1 tablespoon minced garlic
2 cans (10½ ounces each)
 beef broth
1 bottle (12 ounces) beer
 Crusty French rolls,
 sliced in half

1. Trim excess fat from beef and discard. Place beef in **CROCK-POT**® slow cooker.

2. Combine soup mix, sugar, oregano, garlic, broth and beer in large mixing bowl. Pour mixture over beef. Cover; cook on HIGH 6 to 8 hours or until beef is fork-tender.

3. Remove beef from **CROCK-POT**® slow cooker. Shred beef with two forks. Return beef to cooking liquid; mix well. Serve on crusty rolls with extra cooking liquid ("jus") on side for dipping.

Makes 8 to 10 servings

Slow Cooker Stuffed Peppers

1. Set aside seasoning packet from rice. Combine rice mix, beef, celery, onion and egg in large bowl. Divide meat mixture evenly among bell pepper halves.

2. Pour tomatoes with juice into **CROCK-POT®** slow cooker. Arrange filled bell pepper halves on top of tomatoes.

3. Combine tomato soup, water and reserved rice-mix seasoning packet in medium bowl. Pour over bell peppers. Cover; cook on LOW 8 to 10 hours.

Makes 4 servings

1 package (about 7 ounces)
  Spanish rice mix
1 pound lean ground beef
½ cup diced celery
1 small onion, chopped
1 egg, beaten
4 medium green bell
  peppers, halved
  lengthwise, cored and
  seeded
1 can (28 ounces) whole
  peeled tomatoes,
  undrained
1 can (10¾ ounces)
  condensed tomato
  soup, undiluted
1 cup water

1 tablespoon vegetable oil
1 beef brisket (3 to 4 pounds)
1 tablespoon garlic powder, divided
1 tablespoon salt, divided
1 tablespoon black pepper, divided
1 teaspoon paprika, divided
5 to 6 new potatoes, cut into quarters
4 to 5 medium onions, sliced
1 pound baby carrots
1 can (14½ ounces) beef broth

Slow-Cooked Pot Roast

1. Heat oil on HIGH in **CROCK-POT**® slow cooker. Brown brisket on all sides. Transfer brisket to plate. Season with 1½ teaspoons garlic powder, 1½ teaspoons salt, 1½ teaspoons pepper and ½ teaspoon paprika; set aside.

2. Season potatoes with remaining 1½ teaspoons garlic powder, 1½ teaspoons salt, 1½ teaspoons pepper and ½ teaspoon paprika. Add potatoes and onions to **CROCK-POT**® slow cooker. Cook on HIGH, stirring occasionally, until browned.

3. Return brisket to **CROCK-POT**® slow cooker. Add carrots and broth. Cover; cook on HIGH 4 to 5 hours or on LOW 8 to 10 hours, or until beef is tender.

Makes 6 to 8 servings

Round Steak

1. Place steak in large resealable plastic food storage bag. Close bag and pound with meat mallet to tenderize steak. Combine flour, 1 teaspoon pepper and ½ teaspoon salt in small bowl; add to bag with steaks. Shake to coat meat evenly.

2. Heat oil in large skillet over medium-high heat until hot. Remove steak from bag; shake off excess flour. Add steak to skillet; brown both sides. Transfer steak and pan juices to **CROCK-POT®** slow cooker.

3. Add canned soup, water, onion, mushrooms, milk, dry soup mix, bay leaf and seasonings, to taste, to **CROCK-POT®** slow cooker; mix well. Cover; cook on LOW 5 to 6 hours or until steak is tender. Remove and discard bay leaf before serving.

Makes 4 servings

1 boneless beef round steak (1½ pounds), trimmed and cut into 4 pieces
¼ cup all-purpose flour
1 teaspoon black pepper
½ teaspoon salt
1 tablespoon vegetable oil
1 can (10¾ ounces) condensed cream of mushroom soup, undiluted
¾ cup water
1 medium onion, quartered
1 can (4 ounces) sliced mushrooms, drained
¼ cup milk
1 package (1 ounce) dry onion soup mix
1 bay leaf
Seasonings to taste: salt, black pepper, ground sage, dried thyme

Shredded Beef Fajitas

1 beef flank steak (about 1½ pounds)
1 can (14½ ounces) diced tomatoes with jalapeños, undrained
1 cup chopped onion
1 medium green bell pepper, cut into ½-inch pieces
2 cloves garlic, minced *or* ¼ teaspoon garlic powder
1 package (about 1½ ounces) fajita seasoning mix
12 (8-inch) flour tortillas
Optional toppings: reduced-fat sour cream, guacamole, shredded reduced-fat Cheddar cheese, salsa

1. Cut flank steak into 6 portions; place in **CROCK-POT**® slow cooker. Combine tomatoes with juice, onion, bell pepper, garlic and fajita seasoning mix in medium bowl. Pour over steak. Cover; cook on LOW 8 to 10 hours or on HIGH 4 to 5 hours, or until beef is tender.

2. Remove beef from **CROCK-POT**® slow cooker; shred with two forks. Return beef to **CROCK-POT**® slow cooker and stir.

3. To serve fajitas, place meat mixture evenly into flour tortillas. Add toppings as desired; roll up tortillas.

Makes 12 servings

Classic Beef and Noodles

1. Heat oil in large skillet over medium heat until hot. Brown beef on all sides. (Work in batches, if necessary.) Drain fat and discard.

2. Combine beef, mushrooms, onion, garlic, salt, oregano, pepper, marjoram and bay leaf in **CROCK-POT®** slow cooker. Pour in broth and sherry. Cover; cook on LOW 8 to 10 hours or on HIGH 4 to 5 hours. Remove bay leaf and discard.

3. Combine sour cream, flour and water in small bowl. Stir about 1 cup cooking liquid from **CROCK-POT®** slow cooker into sour cream mixture. Add mixture to **CROCK-POT®** slow cooker; mix well. Cook, uncovered, on HIGH 30 minutes or until thickened and bubbly. Serve over noodles.

Makes 8 servings

1 tablespoon vegetable oil
2 pounds beef for stew, cut into 1-inch pieces
¼ pound fresh mushrooms, sliced into halves
2 tablespoons chopped onion
2 cloves garlic, minced
1 teaspoon salt
1 teaspoon dried oregano
½ teaspoon black pepper
¼ teaspoon dried marjoram
1 bay leaf
1½ cups beef broth
⅓ cup dry sherry
1 cup (8 ounces) sour cream
½ cup all-purpose flour
¼ cup water
4 cups hot cooked noodles

Burgundy Beef Po' Boys with Dipping Sauce

1 boneless beef chuck shoulder or bottom round roast (3 pounds)
2 cups chopped onions
¼ cup dry red wine
3 tablespoons balsamic vinegar
1 tablespoon beef bouillon granules
1 tablespoon Worcestershire sauce
¾ teaspoon dried thyme
½ teaspoon garlic powder
Italian rolls, warmed and sliced in half

1. Trim excess fat from beef and discard. Cut beef into 3 or 4 pieces. Place onions on bottom of **CROCK-POT**® slow cooker. Top with beef and remaining ingredients, except rolls. Cover; cook on HIGH 8 to 10 hours or until beef is very tender.

2. Remove beef from **CROCK-POT**® slow cooker; cool slightly. Trim and discard fat from beef. Shred beef with two forks. Let cooking liquid stand 5 minutes to allow fat to rise. Skim off fat and discard.

3. Spoon beef into rolls and serve cooking liquid as dipping sauce.

Makes 6 to 8 sandwiches

Spicy Italian Beef

1. Trim fat from beef and discard. Cut beef, if necessary, to fit in **CROCK-POT®** slow cooker, leaving beef in as many large pieces as possible.

2. Drain pepperoncini; pull off stem ends and discard. Add pepperoncini, broth, beer, onion and herb blend to **CROCK-POT®** slow cooker; do not stir. Cover; cook on LOW 8 to 10 hours.

3. Remove beef from **CROCK-POT®** slow cooker; shred with two forks. Return shredded beef to cooking liquid; mix well. Serve on French bread, topped with cheese, if desired. Serve with additional sauce and pepperoncini, if desired.

Makes 8 to 10 servings

Tip: Pepperoncini are thin, 2- to 3-inch-long pickled mild peppers, available in the supermarket's Italian foods or pickled foods section.

1 boneless beef chuck
   roast (3 to 4 pounds)
1 jar (12 ounces)
   pepperoncini
1 can (14½ ounces) beef
   broth
1 bottle (12 ounces) beer
1 onion, minced
2 tablespoons dried Italian
   seasoning
1 loaf French bread, cut
   into thick slices
10 slices provolone cheese
   (optional)

Yankee Pot Roast and Vegetables

1 beef chuck pot roast
    (about 2½ pounds)
    Salt and black pepper
3 unpeeled medium
    baking potatoes
    (about 1 pound), cut
    into quarters
2 large carrots, cut into
    ¾-inch slices
2 ribs celery, cut into
    ¾-inch slices
1 medium onion, sliced
1 large parsnip, cut into
    ¾-inch slices
2 bay leaves
1 teaspoon dried rosemary
½ teaspoon dried thyme
½ cup reduced-sodium
    beef broth

1. Trim excess fat from beef and discard. Cut beef into serving-size pieces; sprinkle with salt and pepper.

2. Combine potatoes, carrots, celery, onion, parsnip, bay leaves, rosemary and thyme in **CROCK-POT**® slow cooker. Place beef over vegetables. Pour broth over beef. Cover; cook on LOW 8½ to 9 hours, or until beef is fork-tender.

3. Transfer beef to serving platter. Arrange vegetables around beef. Remove and discard bay leaves before serving.

Makes 10 to 12 servings

Tip: To make gravy, ladle cooking liquid into 2-cup measure; let stand 5 minutes. Skim off fat and discard. Measure remaining cooking liquid and heat to a boil in small saucepan. For each cup of cooking liquid, mix 2 tablespoons flour with ¼ cup cold water until smooth. Stir flour mixture into boiling cooking liquid, stirring constantly 1 minute or until thickened.

Osso Bucco

1. Coat **CROCK-POT**® slow cooker with nonstick cooking spray. Place onion, carrots and sliced garlic in bottom. Arrange veal shanks over vegetables, overlapping slightly, and sprinkle herbs, salt and pepper over all. Add consommé and vermouth, if desired. Cover; cook on LOW 8 to 9 hours or on HIGH 5 to 6 hours, or until shanks and vegetables are tender.

2. Transfer shanks and vegetables to serving platter; cover with foil to keep warm. Turn **CROCK-POT**® slow cooker to HIGH. Combine flour with 3 tablespoons water, mixing until smooth. Stir into cooking liquid. Cover; cook on HIGH 15 minutes or until sauce thickens.

3. Serve sauce over shanks and vegetables. Combine parsley, minced garlic and lemon peel; sprinkle over shanks and vegetables.

Makes 4 servings

1 large onion, cut into thin wedges
2 large carrots, sliced
4 cloves garlic, sliced
4 meaty veal shanks (3 to 4 pounds)
2 teaspoons herbs d'Provence *or* ½ teaspoon each dried thyme, rosemary, oregano and basil
1 teaspoon salt
½ teaspoon black pepper
¾ cup canned beef consommé *or* beef broth
¼ cup dry vermouth (optional)
3 tablespoons flour
¼ cup minced parsley
1 small clove garlic, minced
1 teaspoon grated lemon peel

1 boneless beef chuck
    roast (about 3 pounds)
¼ cup ketchup
2 tablespoons brown
    sugar
2 tablespoons red wine
    vinegar
1 tablespoon Dijon
    mustard
1 tablespoon
    Worcestershire sauce
1 clove garlic, crushed
¼ teaspoon salt
¼ teaspoon liquid smoke
⅛ teaspoon black pepper
10 to 12 French rolls or
    sandwich buns, sliced
    in half

BBQ Beef Sandwiches

1. Place beef in **CROCK-POT®** slow cooker. Combine remaining ingredients, except rolls, in medium bowl; pour over meat. Cover; cook on LOW 8 to 9 hours.

2. Remove beef from **CROCK-POT®** slow cooker; shred with two forks.

3. Combine beef with 1 cup sauce from **CROCK-POT®** slow cooker. Evenly distribute meat and sauce mixture among warmed rolls.

Makes 10 to 12 servings

Dilly Beef Sandwiches

1. Trim excess fat from beef and discard. Cut beef into chunks. Place in **CROCK-POT**® slow cooker.

2. Pour pickles with juice over beef. Add tomatoes, onion, garlic and mustard seeds. Cover; cook on LOW 8 to 10 hours.

3. Remove beef from **CROCK-POT**® slow cooker. Shred beef with two forks. Return beef to tomato mixture; mix well. Serve on toasted hamburger buns.

Makes 6 to 8 servings

1 chuck beef roast (3 to 4 pounds)
1 jar (6 ounces) sliced dill pickles, undrained
1 can (14 ounces) crushed tomatoes with Italian seasoning
1 medium onion, diced
4 cloves garlic, minced
1 teaspoon mustard seeds
  Hamburger buns
  Optional toppings: lettuce, sliced tomatoes, sliced red onions, shredded slaw

Slow Cooker Brisket of Beef

1 whole well-trimmed
   beef brisket (about
   5 pounds)
2 teaspoons minced garlic
½ teaspoon black pepper
2 large onions, cut into
   ¼-inch slices and
   separated into rings
1 bottle (12 ounces) chili
   sauce
12 ounces beef broth, dark
   ale *or* water
2 tablespoons
   Worcestershire sauce
1 tablespoon packed
   brown sugar

1. Place brisket, fat side down, in **CROCK-POT**® slow cooker. Spread garlic evenly over brisket; sprinkle with pepper. Arrange onions over brisket. Combine chili sauce, broth, Worcestershire sauce and sugar in medium bowl; pour over brisket and onions. Cover; cook on LOW 8 hours.

2. Turn brisket over; stir onions into sauce and spoon over brisket. Cover; cook on LOW 1 to 2 hours or until brisket is fork-tender. Transfer brisket to cutting board; cover with foil to keep warm. Let stand 10 minutes.

3. Stir cooking liquid, then let stand 5 minutes to allow fat to rise. Skim off fat and discard. (Cooking liquid may be thinned to desired consistency with water or thickened by simmering, uncovered, in saucepan.) Carve brisket across grain into thin slices. Spoon cooking liquid over brisket.

Makes 10 to 12 servings

Roast Beef Burritos

1. Place roast in **CROCK-POT®** slow cooker; add water. Season with garlic powder and pepper to taste. Add bay leaf. Cover; cook on HIGH 6 hours or until beef is tender. Remove bay leaf and discard.

2. Transfer beef to cutting board. Trim fat from beef and discard. Shred beef with two forks. Let cooking liquid stand 5 minutes to allow fat to rise. Skim off fat and discard. Add shredded beef, salsa, chilies and onion to cooking liquid in **CROCK-POT®** slow cooker; stir to combine. Cover; cook on HIGH 1 hour or until onion is tender.

3. To serve, place about 3 tablespoons beef onto each tortilla. Top with cheese and fold into burritos. Place burrito, seam-side-down, on plate. Microwave 30 seconds to melt cheese. Serve with extra salsa, if desired.

Makes 8 to 10 servings

1 boneless beef rump or bottom round roast (3 to 5 pounds)
¼ cup water
½ to 1 teaspoon garlic powder
½ to 1 teaspoon black pepper
1 bay leaf
2 jars (16 ounces each) salsa, plus extra for garnish
2 cans (4 ounces each) diced green chilies, undrained
½ large yellow onion, diced
8 to 10 burrito-size flour tortillas
1 cup shredded Cheddar cheese

Seafood Specialties

Creamy Slow Cooker Seafood Chowder

1 quart (4 cups) half-and-half
2 cans (14½ ounces each) whole white potatoes, drained and cubed
2 cans (10¾ ounces) condensed cream of mushroom soup, undiluted
1 bag (16 ounces) frozen hash brown potatoes
1 medium onion, minced
½ cup (1 stick) butter, diced
1 teaspoon salt
1 teaspoon black pepper
5 cans (about 8 ounces each) whole oysters, drained and rinsed
2 cans (about 6 ounces each) minced clams
2 cans (about 4 ounces each) cocktail shrimp, drained and rinsed

1. Combine half-and-half, canned potatoes, soup, frozen potatoes, onion, butter, salt and pepper in 5- or 6-quart **CROCK-POT®** slow cooker. Mix well.

2. Cover; cook on LOW 3 to 4 hours.

3. Add oysters, clams and shrimp; stir gently. Cover; cook on LOW 30 to 45 minutes or until seafood is done.

Makes 8 to 10 servings

1 package (12 ounces)
  frozen shrimp, thawed
½ cup chicken broth
1 clove garlic, minced
1 teaspoon chili powder
½ teaspoon salt
½ teaspoon dried oregano
1 cup frozen peas, thawed
½ cup diced tomatoes
2 cups cooked long-grain
  white rice

Caribbean Shrimp with Rice

1. Combine shrimp, broth, garlic, chili powder, salt and oregano in **CROCK-POT®** slow cooker. Cover; cook on LOW 2 hours.

2. Add peas and tomatoes. Cover; cook on LOW 5 minutes.

3. Stir in rice. Cover; cook on LOW an additional 5 minutes.

Makes 4 servings

Sweet and Sour Shrimp with Pineapple

1. Drain pineapple chunks, reserving 1 cup juice. Place pineapple and snow peas in **CROCK-POT**® slow cooker.

2. Combine cornstarch and sugar in medium saucepan. Dissolve bouillon cubes in water and add to saucepan. Mix in 1 cup reserved pineapple juice, soy sauce and ginger. Bring to a boil and cook for 1 minute. Pour into **CROCK-POT**® slow cooker. Cover; cook on LOW 4½ to 5½ hours.

3. Add shrimp and vinegar. Cover; cook on LOW 30 minutes or until shrimp are done. Serve over hot rice.

Makes 4 servings

3 cans (8 ounces each) pineapple chunks, drained, 1 cup juice reserved
2 packages (6 ounces each) frozen snow peas, thawed
¼ cup cornstarch
⅓ cup sugar, plus 2 teaspoons
2 chicken bouillon cubes
2 cups boiling water
4 teaspoons soy sauce
1 teaspoon ground ginger
1 pound shrimp, peeled, deveined and cleaned
¼ cup cider vinegar
Hot cooked rice

1 can (28 ounces) diced tomatoes, undrained
1 medium onion, chopped
1 medium red bell pepper, chopped
1 rib celery, chopped (about ½ cup)
2 tablespoons minced garlic
2 teaspoons dried parsley flakes
2 teaspoons dried oregano
1 teaspoon hot pepper sauce
½ teaspoon dried thyme
2 pounds cooked large shrimp
2 cups uncooked instant rice
2 cups chicken broth

Shrimp Jambalaya

1. Combine tomatoes with juice, onion, bell pepper, celery, garlic, parsley, oregano, hot sauce and thyme in **CROCK-POT®** slow cooker. Cover; cook on LOW 8 hours or on HIGH 4 hours.

2. Stir in shrimp. Cover; cook on LOW 20 minutes.

3. Meanwhile, prepare rice according to package directions, substituting broth for water. Serve jambalaya over hot cooked rice.

Makes 6 servings

Peachy Sweet and Sour Shrimp

1. Place peaches with syrup, onions, bell peppers, celery, broth, sesame oil, soy sauce, vinegar and pepper flakes in **CROCK-POT®** slow cooker. Cover; cook on LOW 3 to 4 hours or on HIGH 2 to 3 hours or until vegetables are tender. Stir well.

2. Blend cornstarch and water, and mix into vegetable mixture. Add snow peas. Cover; cook on HIGH 15 minutes or until thickened.

3. Add shrimp, tomatoes and walnuts. Cover; cook on HIGH 4 to 5 minutes or until shrimp is hot. Serve with rice, if desired.

Makes 4 to 6 servings

1 can (about 16 ounces) sliced peaches in syrup, undrained
½ cup chopped green onions
½ cup chopped red bell pepper
½ cup chopped green bell pepper
½ cup sliced celery
⅓ cup vegetable broth
2 tablespoons dark sesame oil
¼ cup light soy sauce
2 tablespoons rice wine vinegar
1 teaspoon red pepper flakes
2 tablespoons cornstarch
¼ cup water
1 package (6 ounces) frozen snow peas, thawed
1 pound cooked medium shrimp
1 cup cherry tomatoes, cut into halves
½ cup toasted walnut pieces

Shrimp Creole

¼ cup (½ stick) butter
1 onion, chopped
¼ cup biscuit baking mix
3 cups water
1 cup chopped celery
1 cup chopped green bell
   pepper
2 cans (6 ounces each)
   tomato paste
2 teaspoons salt
½ teaspoon sugar
2 bay leaves
   Black pepper, to taste
4 pounds shrimp, peeled,
   deveined and cleaned
   Hot cooked rice

1. Cook and stir butter and onion in medium skillet until onion is tender. Stir in biscuit mix. Place mixture in **CROCK-POT**® slow cooker.

2. Add water, celery, bell pepper, tomato paste, salt, sugar, bay leaves and black pepper. Cover; cook on LOW 6 to 8 hours.

3. Turn **CROCK-POT**® slow cooker to HIGH and add shrimp. Cook 45 minutes to 1 hour or until shrimp are done. Remove bay leaves. Serve over rice.

Makes 8 to 10 servings

Cream of Scallop Soup

1. Combine potatoes, water, milk, onions, carrots, broth, wine, garlic powder and thyme in **CROCK-POT®** slow cooker. Cover; cook on LOW 6 to 8 hours or HIGH 3 to 5 hours.

2. Turn **CROCK-POT®** slow cooker to LOW and mix in egg yolks. Cover; cook 1 hour.

3. Add scallops and cook, uncovered, 10 to 20 minutes. Before serving, mix in cheese and cook, uncovered, 5 minutes or until cheese has melted.

Makes 4 to 6 servings

Tip: Scallops cook very quickly; overcooking will make them tough, so check for doneness early. Small bay scallops will cook more quickly than larger sea scallops.

1½ pounds red potatoes, cubed
3 cups water
1½ cups milk
2 onions, chopped
2 carrots, shredded
½ cup vegetable broth
2 tablespoons white wine
½ teaspoon garlic powder
½ teaspoon dried thyme
2 egg yolks, lightly beaten
1 pound sea scallops
1 cup shredded Cheddar cheese

Manhattan Clam Chowder

3 slices bacon, diced
2 celery stalks, chopped
3 onions, chopped
2 cups water
1 can (15 ounces) stewed
    tomatoes, undrained
    and chopped
4 small red potatoes, diced
2 carrots, diced
½ teaspoon dried thyme
½ teaspoon black pepper
½ teaspoon Louisiana-style
    hot sauce
1 pound minced clams*

If minced clams are unavailable, use canned clams; six 6½-ounce cans yield about 1 pound of clam meat; drain and discard liquid.

1. Cook and stir bacon in medium saucepan until bacon is crisp. Remove bacon and place in **CROCK-POT**® slow cooker.

2. Add celery and onions to skillet. Cook and stir until tender. Place in **CROCK-POT**® slow cooker.

3. Mix in water, tomatoes with juice, potatoes, carrots, thyme, pepper and hot sauce. Cover; cook on LOW 6 to 8 hours or HIGH 4 to 6 hours. Add clams during last hour of cooking.

Makes 4 servings

New England Clam Chowder

1. Cook and stir bacon and onion in medium skillet until onions are tender. Place in **CROCK-POT®** slow cooker.

2. Add enough water to reserved clam liquid to make 3 cups. Pour into **CROCK-POT®** slow cooker, and add potatoes, garlic and pepper. Cover; cook on LOW 5 to 8 hours or HIGH 1 to 3 hours.

3. Turn **CROCK-POT®** slow cooker to LOW and mix in reserved clams and milk. Cover; cook 1 hour. Adjust seasoning, if necessary.

Makes 6 to 8 servings

6 slices bacon, diced
2 onions, chopped
5 cans (6½ ounces each) clams, drained and liquid reserved
6 medium red potatoes, cubed
2 tablespoons minced garlic
1 teaspoon black pepper
2 cans (12 ounces each) evaporated milk
Salt, to taste

Crowd-Pleasing Pork

Pork and Tomato Ragout

2 pounds pork stew meat,
  cut into 1-inch pieces
¼ cup all-purpose flour
3 tablespoons oil
1¼ cups white wine
2 pounds red potatoes, cut
  into ½-inch pieces
1 can (14½ ounces) diced
  tomatoes, undrained
1 cup finely chopped
  onion
1 cup water
½ cup finely chopped
  celery
2 cloves garlic, minced
½ teaspoon black pepper
1 cinnamon stick
3 tablespoons chopped
  fresh parsley

1. Toss pork with flour. Heat oil in large skillet over medium-high heat until hot. Add pork to skillet and brown on all sides. Transfer to **CROCK-POT**® slow cooker.

2. Add wine to skillet; bring to a boil, scraping up browned bits from bottom of skillet. Pour into **CROCK-POT**® slow cooker.

3. Add all remaining ingredients except parsley. Cover; cook on LOW 6 to 8 hours or until pork and potatoes are tender. Remove and discard cinnamon stick. Adjust seasonings, if desired. To serve, sprinkle with parsley.

Makes 6 servings

Scalloped Potatoes and Ham

6 large russet potatoes,
    sliced into ¼-inch
    rounds
1 ham steak (about
    1½ pounds), cut into
    cubes
1 can (10¾ ounces)
    condensed cream of
    mushroom soup,
    undiluted
1 soup can water
1 cup shredded Cheddar
    cheese
    Grill seasoning, to taste

1. Layer potatoes and ham in **CROCK-POT**® slow cooker.

2. Combine soup, water, cheese and seasoning in large mixing bowl. Pour mixture over potatoes and ham.

3. Cover; cook on HIGH 3½ hours or until potatoes are fork-tender. Turn **CROCK-POT**® slow cooker to LOW and continue cooking 1 hour.

Makes 5 to 6 servings

Italian Sausage and Peppers

1. Coat **CROCK-POT**® slow cooker with nonstick cooking spray. Place bell peppers, onion and garlic in **CROCK-POT**® slow cooker. Arrange sausage over vegetables. Combine pasta sauce and wine; pour over sausage. Cover; cook on LOW 8 to 9 hours on HIGH 4 to 5 hours or until sausage is cooked through and vegetables are very tender.

2. Transfer sausage to serving platter; cover with foil to keep warm. Skim off and discard fat from cooking liquid.

3. Turn heat to HIGH. Mix cornstarch with water until smooth; add to **CROCK-POT**® slow cooker. Cook 15 minutes or until sauce has thickened, stirring once. Serve sauce over spaghetti and sausage; top with cheese.

Makes 4 servings

3 cups bell pepper chunks (1 inch), preferably a mix of red, yellow and green*
1 small onion, cut into thin wedges
3 cloves garlic, minced
4 links hot or mild Italian sausage (about 1 pound)
1 cup marinara or pasta sauce
¼ cup red wine or port
1 tablespoon cornstarch
1 tablespoon water
Hot cooked spaghetti
¼ cup shredded Parmesan or Romano cheese

Look for mixed bell pepper chunks at supermarket salad bars.

Vegetable-Stuffed Pork Chops

4 double pork rib chops, well trimmed

Salt and black pepper, to taste

1 can (15¼ ounces) kernel corn, drained

1 green bell pepper, chopped

1 cup Italian-style seasoned dry bread crumbs

1 small onion, chopped

½ cup uncooked converted long-grain rice

1 can (8 ounces) tomato sauce

1. Cut pocket into each pork chop, cutting from edge nearest bone. Lightly season pockets with salt and pepper to taste. Combine corn, bell pepper, bread crumbs, onion and rice in large bowl. Stuff pork chops with rice mixture. Secure open side with toothpicks.

2. Place any remaining rice mixture in **CROCK-POT®** slow cooker. Add stuffed pork chops to **CROCK-POT®** slow cooker. Moisten top of each pork chop with tomato sauce. Pour in any remaining tomato sauce. Cover; cook on LOW 8 to 10 hours.

3. Transfer pork chops to serving platter. Remove and discard toothpicks. Serve pork chops with extra rice mixture.

Makes 4 servings

Spicy Asian Pork Filling

1. Cut roast into 2- to 3-inch chunks. Combine pork, tamari sauce, chili garlic sauce and ginger in **CROCK-POT**® slow cooker; mix well. Cover; cook on LOW 8 to 10 hours or until pork is fork-tender.

2. Remove roast from cooking liquid; cool slightly. Trim excess fat from meat and discard. Shred pork with two forks. Let cooking liquid stand 5 minutes to allow fat to rise. Skim off and discard fat from cooking liquid.

3. Blend water, cornstarch and sesame oil until smooth; stir into **CROCK-POT**® slow cooker. Cook, uncovered, on HIGH until thickened. Add shredded meat to **CROCK-POT**® slow cooker; mix well. Cover; cook 15 to 30 minutes or until hot.

Makes 5½ cups filling

Spicy Asian Pork Bundles: Place ¼ cup pork filling into large lettuce leaves. Add shredded carrots, if desired. Wrap to enclose. Makes about 20 bundles.

Mu Shu Pork: Lightly spread prepared plum sauce over small warm flour tortillas. Spoon ¼ cup pork filling and ¼ cup stir-fried vegetables into flour tortillas. Wrap to enclose. Serve immediately. Makes about 20 wraps.

1 boneless pork sirloin roast (about 3 pounds)
½ cup tamari or other soy sauce
1 tablespoon chili garlic sauce *or* chili paste
2 teaspoons minced fresh ginger
2 tablespoons water
1 tablespoon cornstarch
2 teaspoons dark sesame oil

Barbecued Pulled Pork Sandwiches

1 pork shoulder roast
   (about 2½ pounds)
1 bottle (14 ounces)
   barbecue sauce
1 tablespoon fresh lemon
   juice
1 teaspoon brown sugar
1 medium onion, chopped
8 hamburger buns or hard
   rolls

1. Place pork roast in **CROCK-POT**® slow cooker. Cover; cook on LOW 10 to 12 hours or on HIGH 5 to 6 hours.

2. Remove pork roast from **CROCK-POT**® slow cooker; discard cooking liquid. Shred pork with two forks. Return pork to **CROCK-POT**® slow cooker. Add barbecue sauce, lemon juice, brown sugar and onion. Cover; cook on LOW 2 hours or on HIGH 1 hour.

3. Serve shredded pork on hamburger buns or hard rolls.

Makes 8 servings

Tip: For 5-, 6- or 7-quart **CROCK-POT**® slow cooker, double all ingredients, except barbecue sauce. Increase barbecue sauce to 21 ounces.

Pork Loin with Sherry and Red Onions

1. Cook and stir red onions and pearl onions in butter in a medium skillet until tender.

2. Rub pork loin with salt and pepper and place in **CROCK-POT**® slow cooker. Add cooked onions, sherry and parsley. Cover; cook on LOW 8 to 10 hours or on HIGH 5 to 6 hours.

3. Remove pork loin from **CROCK-POT**® slow cooker; let stand 15 minutes before slicing. Meanwhile, combine cornstarch and water. Stir into cooking liquid and cook on LOW until sauce has thickened. Serve pork loin with onions and sherry sauce.

Makes 8 servings

Tip: For 5-, 6- or 7-quart **CROCK-POT**® slow cooker, double all ingredients, except sherry, cornstarch and water.

3 large red onions, thinly sliced
1 cup pearl onions, blanched and peeled
2 tablespoons unsalted butter or margarine
2½ pounds boneless pork loin, tied
½ teaspoon salt
½ teaspoon black pepper
½ cup cooking sherry
2 tablespoons Italian parsley, chopped
1½ tablespoons cornstarch
2 tablespoons water

Pork Chops with Jalapeño-Pecan Cornbread Stuffing

6 boneless loin pork
   chops, 1 inch thick
   (1½ pounds)
¾ cup chopped onion
¾ cup chopped celery
½ cup coarsely chopped
   pecans
½ medium jalapeño
   pepper, seeded and
   chopped
1 teaspoon rubbed sage
½ teaspoon dried rosemary
⅛ teaspoon black pepper
4 cups unseasoned
   cornbread stuffing
   mix
1¼ cups reduced-sodium
   chicken broth
1 egg, lightly beaten

1. Trim excess fat from pork and discard. Coat large skillet with nonstick cooking spray; heat over medium heat until hot. Add pork; cook 10 minutes or until browned on both sides. Remove; set aside.

2. Add onion, celery, pecans, jalapeño pepper, sage, rosemary and black pepper to skillet. Cook 5 minutes or until onion and celery are tender.

3. Combine cornbread stuffing mix, vegetable mixture and broth in medium bowl. Stir in egg. Spoon stuffing mixture into **CROCK-POT®** slow cooker. Arrange pork on top. Cover; cook on LOW about 5 hours or until pork is tender.

Makes 6 servings

Note: For moister dressing, increase chicken broth to 1½ cups.

Slow Cooker Cassoulet

1. Rinse and sort beans and place in large bowl; cover completely with water. Soak 6 to 8 hours or overnight. (To quick-soak beans, place beans in large saucepan; cover with water. Bring to a boil over high heat. Boil 2 minutes. Remove from heat; let soak, covered, 1 hour.) Drain beans; discard water.

2. Heat butter and oil in large skillet over medium-high heat until hot. Sear shanks on all sides until browned. Transfer to **CROCK-POT**® slow cooker. Add broth, bacon, garlic, beans, herbs, and cloves. Add enough water to cover beans, if needed. Cover; cook on LOW 8 hours. After about 4 hours, check liquid and add boiling water as needed.

3. Before serving, season with salt and pepper. Grill sausages and serve with cassoulet.

Makes 4 servings

1 pound white beans, such as Great Northern
 Boiling water to cover beans
1 tablespoon butter
1 tablespoon canola oil
4 veal shanks, 1½ inches thick, tied for cooking
3 cups beef broth
4 ounces maple-smoked bacon or pancetta, diced
3 cloves garlic, smashed
1 sprig each thyme and savory (*or* a bouquet garni of 1 tablespoon each)
2 whole cloves
 Salt and pepper, to taste
4 mild Italian sausages

Fall-Off-the-Bone BBQ Ribs

½ cup paprika
⅜ cup sugar
¼ cup onion powder
1½ teaspoons salt
1½ teaspoons black pepper
2½ pounds pork baby back ribs, skinned
1 can (20 ounces) beer or beef stock
1 quart barbecue sauce
½ cup honey
   White sesame seeds and chives for garnish (optional)

1. Lightly oil grill grate and preheat on HIGH.

2. While grill heats, combine paprika, sugar, onion powder, salt and pepper in large mixing bowl. Generously season ribs with dry rub mixture. Place ribs on grill. Cook for 3 minutes on each side or until ribs have grill marks.

3. Portion racks into sections of 3 to 4 bones. Place in 5-quart **CROCK-POT**® slow cooker. Pour beer over ribs. Cover; cook on HIGH 2 hours. Blend barbecue sauce and honey; add to **CROCK-POT**® slow cooker. Cover; cook on HIGH for 1½ hours. Garnish with white sesame seeds and chives, if desired. Serve with extra sauce on the side.

Makes 6 to 8 servings

Company Slow Cooker Pork Chops

1. Blend soup, milk, cream cheese and sour cream until smooth. Heat oil in large skillet over medium-high heat until hot. Brown pork chops on both sides. Season with pepper.

2. Coat **CROCK-POT**® slow cooker with nonstick cooking spray. Place half of pork chops into **CROCK-POT**® slow cooker. Top with 4 slices dried beef. Pour half of sauce mixture over pork. Repeat with remaining chops, dried beef and sauce.

3. Cover; cook on LOW 8 to 9 hours. Adjust seasoning before serving, if necessary.

Makes 4 to 6 servings

2 cans (10¾ ounces each) condensed fat-free cream of mushroom soup, undiluted
½ cup skim milk
1 package (3 ounces) low-fat cream cheese, softened
¼ cup fat-free sour cream
2 tablespoons oil
4 to 6 pork loin chops, cut ¾ inch thick
Black pepper, to taste
1 jar (2½ ounces) sliced dried beef

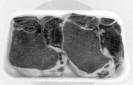

Sauerkraut Pork Ribs

1 tablespoon vegetable oil
3 to 4 pounds pork country-style ribs
1 large onion, thinly sliced
1 teaspoon caraway seeds
½ teaspoon garlic powder
¼ to ½ teaspoon black pepper
¾ cup water
2 jars (about 28 ounces each) sauerkraut
12 medium red potatoes, quartered

1. Heat oil in large skillet over medium-low heat until hot. Brown ribs on all sides. Transfer to **CROCK-POT®** slow cooker. Drain excess fat and discard.

2. Add onion to skillet; cook until tender. Add caraway seeds, garlic powder and pepper; cook 15 minutes. Transfer onion mixture to **CROCK-POT®** slow cooker.

3. Add water to skillet and scrape up any browned bits. Pour pan juices into **CROCK-POT®** slow cooker. Partially drain sauerkraut, leaving some liquid; pour over meat. Top with potatoes. Cover; cook on LOW 6 to 8 hours or until potatoes are tender, stirring once during cooking.

Makes 12 servings

Lemon Pork Chops

1. Heat oil in large skillet over medium-low heat until hot. Brown pork chops on both sides. Drain excess fat and discard. Place pork chops into **CROCK-POT**® slow cooker.

2. Combine tomato sauce, onion, if desired, bell pepper, lemon-pepper seasoning and Worcestershire, and add to **CROCK-POT**® slow cooker.

3. Squeeze juice from lemon quarters over mixture; drop squeezed peels into **CROCK-POT**® slow cooker. Cover; cook on LOW 6 to 8 hours or until pork is tender. Remove lemon wedges before serving. Garnish with additional lemon wedges, if desired.

Makes 4 servings

1 tablespoon vegetable oil
4 boneless pork chops
3 cans (8 ounces each) tomato sauce
1 large onion, quartered and sliced (optional)
1 large green bell pepper, cut into strips
1 tablespoon lemon-pepper seasoning
1 tablespoon Worcestershire sauce
1 large lemon, quartered Lemon wedges (optional)

Poultry in a Pot

Chicken with Italian Sausage

10 ounces bulk mild or hot Italian sausage
6 boneless skinless chicken thighs
1 can (about 15 ounces) white beans, rinsed and drained
1 can (about 15 ounces) red beans, rinsed and drained
1 cup chicken broth
1 medium onion, chopped
1 teaspoon black pepper
½ teaspoon salt
   Chopped fresh parsley

1. Brown sausage in large skillet over medium-high heat, stirring to break up meat. Drain fat and discard. Spoon sausage into **CROCK-POT®** slow cooker.

2. Trim fat from chicken and discard. Place chicken, beans, broth, onion, pepper and salt in **CROCK-POT®** slow cooker. Cover; cook on LOW 5 to 6 hours.

3. Adjust seasonings, if desired. Slice each chicken thigh on the diagonal. Serve with sausage and beans. Garnish with parsley.

Makes 6 servings

1 tablespoon dried
  oregano
1 teaspoon salt, divided
1 teaspoon paprika
½ teaspoon garlic powder
¼ teaspoon black pepper
2 medium green bell
  peppers, cut into thin
  strips
1 small yellow onion,
  thinly sliced
1 cut-up whole chicken
  (about 3 pounds)
⅓ cup ketchup
  Hot cooked egg noodles

Old World Chicken and Vegetables

1. Combine oregano, ½ teaspoon salt, paprika, garlic powder and black pepper in small bowl; mix well.

2. Place bell peppers and onion in **CROCK-POT**® slow cooker. Add chicken thighs and legs and sprinkle with half of oregano mixture. Add chicken breasts and sprinkle on remaining oregano mixture. Cover; cook on LOW 8 hours or on HIGH 4 hours. Stir in ketchup and remaining ½ teaspoon salt.

3. Serve chicken and vegetables over noodles.

Makes 4 servings

Easy Parmesan Chicken

1. Place mushrooms and onion in **CROCK-POT**® slow cooker.

2. Heat oil in large skillet over medium-high heat until hot. Lightly brown chicken on both sides. Place chicken in **CROCK-POT**® slow cooker. Pour pasta sauce over chicken; add basil, oregano and bay leaf. Cover; cook on LOW 6 to 7 hours or on HIGH 3 to 4 hours or until chicken is tender. Remove and discard bay leaf.

3. Sprinkle chicken with cheeses. Cook, uncovered, on LOW 15 to 30 minutes or until cheeses have melted. Serve over spaghetti.

Makes 4 servings

8 ounces mushrooms, sliced
1 medium onion, cut in thin wedges
1 tablespoon olive oil
4 boneless skinless chicken breasts
1 jar (26 ounces) pasta sauce
½ teaspoon dried basil
¼ teaspoon dried oregano
1 bay leaf
½ cup (2 ounces) shredded part-skim mozzarella cheese
¼ cup grated Parmesan cheese
Hot cooked spaghetti

Fresh Herbed Turkey Breast

2 tablespoons butter, softened
¼ cup fresh sage, minced
¼ cup fresh tarragon, minced
1 clove garlic, minced
1 teaspoon black pepper
½ teaspoon salt
1 split turkey breast (about 4 pounds)
1½ tablespoons cornstarch

1. Combine butter, sage, tarragon, garlic, pepper and salt. Rub butter mixture all over turkey breast.

2. Place turkey breast in **CROCK-POT**® slow cooker. Cover; cook on LOW 8 to 10 hours or on HIGH 4 to 5 hours or until turkey is no longer pink in the center.

3. Transfer turkey breast to serving platter; cover with foil to keep warm. Turn **CROCK-POT**® slow cooker to HIGH; slowly whisk in cornstarch to thicken cooking liquid. When the sauce is thick and smooth, pour over turkey breast. Slice to serve.

Makes 8 servings

Tip: For 5-, 6- or 7-quart **CROCK-POT**® slow cooker, double all ingredients.

Tarragon Turkey & Pasta

1. Combine turkey, celery, green onions, 2 tablespoons fresh tarragon, wine, salt and pepper in **CROCK-POT®** slow cooker. Mix thoroughly. Cover; cook on LOW 6 to 8 hours or on HIGH 3½ to 4 hours or until turkey is no longer pink.

2. Remove turkey and cut it into ½-inch-thick medallions. Turn **CROCK-POT®** slow cooker to HIGH. Add yogurt, remaining 2 tablespoons fresh tarragon, parsley and lemon juice to cooking liquid.

3. Combine cornstarch and water in small bowl. Stir mixture into cooking liquid. Cook until cooking liquid has thickened. Serve turkey medallions and tarragon sauce over pasta.

Makes 4 servings

Tip: For a 5-, 6- or 7-quart **CROCK-POT®** slow cooker, double all ingredients.

1½ to 2 pounds turkey tenderloins
½ cup thinly sliced celery
¼ cup thinly sliced green onions
4 tablespoons fresh tarragon, minced, divided
¼ cup dry white wine
1 teaspoon salt
1 teaspoon black pepper
½ cup plain yogurt
1 tablespoon fresh minced Italian parsley
1 tablespoon lemon juice
1½ tablespoons cornstarch
2 tablespoons water
4 cups hot cooked pasta

2 medium green bell
    peppers, cut into thin
    strips
1 large onion, quartered
    and thinly sliced
4 chicken thighs
4 chicken drumsticks
1 tablespoon chili powder
2 teaspoons dried oregano
1 jar (16 ounces) chipotle
    salsa
½ cup ketchup
2 teaspoons ground cumin
½ teaspoon salt
    Hot cooked noodles

Mexican Chili Chicken

1. Place bell peppers and onion in **CROCK-POT**® slow cooker; top with chicken. Sprinkle chili powder and oregano evenly over chicken. Add salsa. Cover and cook on LOW 7 to 8 hours or on HIGH 2 to 3 hours or until chicken is tender.

2. Transfer chicken to serving bowl; cover with foil to keep warm. Stir ketchup, cumin and salt into cooking liquid. Cook, uncovered, on HIGH 15 minutes or until hot.

3. Pour mixture over chicken. Serve chicken and sauce over noodles.

Tip: For thicker sauce, blend 1 tablespoon cornstarch and 2 tablespoons water. Stir into cooking liquid with ketchup, cumin and salt.

Makes 4 servings

Poultry in a Pot

Autumn Chicken

1. Spread whole artichokes over bottom of **CROCK-POT**® slow cooker. Top with half of mushrooms. Layer chicken over mushrooms. Add marinated artichoke hearts with liquid. Add remaining mushrooms. Pour in wine and vinaigrette.

2. Cover; cook on LOW 4 to 5 hours.

3. Serve chicken and sauce over noodles. Garnish with paprika, if desired.

Makes 10 to 12 servings

1 can (14 ounces) whole artichoke hearts, drained
1 can (14 ounces) whole mushrooms, divided
12 boneless skinless chicken breasts
1 jar (6½ ounces) marinated artichoke hearts, with liquid
¾ cup white wine
½ cup balsamic vinaigrette
Hot cooked noodles
Paprika for garnish (optional)

Country Captain Chicken

4 boneless skinless chicken thighs
2 tablespoons all-purpose flour
2 tablespoons vegetable oil, divided
1 cup chopped green bell pepper
1 large onion, chopped
1 rib celery, chopped
1 clove garlic, minced
¼ cup chicken broth
2 cups canned crushed tomatoes *or* diced fresh tomatoes
½ cup golden raisins
1½ teaspoons curry powder
1 teaspoon salt
¼ teaspoon paprika
¼ teaspoon black pepper
Hot cooked rice
Parsley (optional)

1. Coat chicken with flour; set aside. Heat 1 tablespoon oil in large skillet over medium-high heat until hot. Add bell pepper, onion, celery and garlic. Cook and stir 5 minutes or until vegetables are tender. Place vegetables in **CROCK-POT**® slow cooker.

2. Heat remaining 1 tablespoon oil in same skillet over medium-high heat. Add chicken; cook 5 minutes per side or until browned. Place chicken in **CROCK-POT**® slow cooker.

3. Pour broth into skillet. Cook and stir over medium-high heat, scraping up any browned bits from bottom of skillet. Pour liquid into **CROCK-POT**® slow cooker. Add tomatoes, raisins, curry powder, salt, paprika and black pepper. Cover; cook on LOW 3 hours. Serve chicken and sauce over rice. Garnish with parsley, if desired.

Makes 4 servings

Chicken Sausage with Peppers & Basil

1. Heat olive oil in large skillet over medium heat until hot. Add garlic and onion, and cook until translucent.

2. Remove sausage from casing and cut into 1-inch chunks. Add to skillet and cook 3 to 4 minutes, or until just beginning to brown. Transfer to **CROCK-POT**® slow cooker with slotted spoon, skimming off some fat.

3. Add tomatoes, bell peppers, basil, red pepper flakes, salt and black pepper to **CROCK-POT**® slow cooker, and stir to blend. Cook on HIGH 2½ to 3 hours, or until peppers have softened. Adjust seasonings to taste. Serve over pasta.

Makes 4 servings

Tip: It's not necessary to brown meat before slow cooking. However, if you prefer the look and flavor of browned meat, don't skip this step.

1 tablespoon olive oil
1 clove garlic, minced
½ yellow onion, minced (about ⅓ cup)
1 pound sweet or hot Italian chicken sausage
1 can (28 ounces) whole tomatoes, drained and seeded
½ red bell pepper, cut into ½-inch slices
½ yellow bell pepper, cut into ½-inch slices
½ orange bell pepper, cut into ½-inch slices
¾ cup chopped fresh basil
Crushed red pepper flakes, to taste
Salt and black pepper, to taste
Hot cooked pasta

Thai Chicken

2½ pounds chicken pieces
1 cup hot salsa
¼ cup peanut butter
2 tablespoons lime juice
1 tablespoon soy sauce
1 teaspoon minced fresh
    ginger
Hot cooked rice
½ cup peanuts, chopped
2 tablespoons chopped
    fresh cilantro

1. Place chicken in **CROCK-POT**® slow cooker. Combine salsa, peanut butter, lime juice, soy sauce and ginger; pour over chicken.

2. Cover; cook on LOW 8 to 9 hours or on HIGH 3 to 4 hours or until done.

3. Serve chicken and sauce over rice; sprinkle with peanuts and cilantro.

Makes 6 servings

Mediterranean Chicken

1. Heat oil in large skillet over medium heat until hot. Add chicken and lightly brown on both sides.

2. Combine tomatoes with juice, onions, garlic, sherry, lemon juice, cinnamon, bay leaf and pepper in **CROCK-POT**® slow cooker. Add chicken. Cover; cook on LOW 8 to 10 hours or on HIGH 4 to 5 hours or until done.

3. Remove and discard cinnamon sticks and bay leaf. Serve chicken and sauce over noodles. Sprinkle with cheese just before serving.

Makes 6 servings

1 tablespoon olive oil
2 pounds boneless skinless chicken breasts
1 can (28 ounces) diced tomatoes, undrained
2 onions, chopped
6 teaspoons minced garlic
½ cup sherry
   Juice of 2 lemons
2 cinnamon sticks
1 bay leaf
½ teaspoon black pepper
1 pound hot cooked broad noodles
½ cup feta cheese

Moroccan Chicken Tagine

3 pounds bone-in chicken pieces, skin removed
2 cups chicken broth
1 can (14½ ounces) diced tomatoes, undrained
2 onions, chopped
1 cup dried apricots, chopped
4 cloves garlic, minced
2 teaspoons ground cumin
1 teaspoon ground ginger
1 teaspoon ground cinnamon
½ teaspoon ground coriander
½ teaspoon ground red pepper
6 sprigs fresh cilantro
1 tablespoon cornstarch
1 tablespoon water
1 can (15 ounces) chickpeas, drained and rinsed
2 tablespoons chopped fresh cilantro
¼ cup slivered almonds, toasted
   Hot cooked rice or couscous

1. Place chicken in **CROCK-POT**® slow cooker. Combine broth, tomatoes with juice, onions, apricots, garlic, cumin, ginger, cinnamon, coriander, red pepper and cilantro in medium bowl; pour over chicken. Cover; cook on LOW 4 to 5 hours or until chicken is tender.

2. Transfer chicken to serving platter; cover with foil to keep warm. Combine cornstarch and water in small bowl until smooth. Stir cornstarch mixture and chickpeas into **CROCK-POT**® slow cooker. Cover; cook on HIGH 15 minutes or until sauce has thickened.

3. Pour sauce over chicken. Sprinkle with cilantro and toasted almonds, and serve over rice.

Makes 4 to 6 servings

Tip: To toast almonds, heat small nonstick skillet over medium-high heat. Add almonds; cook and stir about 3 minutes or until golden brown. Remove from pan immediately. Cool before adding to other ingredients.

Chutney Curried Chicken with Yogurt Sauce

1. Place yogurt in paper-towel-lined strainer over a bowl. Drain in refrigerator until serving time.

2. Sprinkle curry powder, garlic salt and red pepper over chicken. Place onion in **CROCK-POT®** slow cooker; top with chicken. Combine chutney, lime juice and garlic; spoon over chicken. Cover; cook on LOW 5 to 6 hours or on HIGH 2½ to 3 hours or until chicken is tender.

3. With slotted spoon, transfer chicken to serving platter; cover with foil to keep warm. Turn **CROCK-POT®** slow cooker to HIGH. Combine cornstarch with water until smooth. Stir into cooking liquid. Cover; cook 15 minutes or until thickened. Spoon sauce over chicken; serve over linguini. Top with thickened yogurt, and garnish as desired.

Makes 4 servings

1 container (6 to 8 ounces) plain low-fat yogurt
2 teaspoons curry powder
1 teaspoon garlic salt
⅛ teaspoon ground red pepper
4 bone-in chicken breast halves, skin removed (2 to 2¼ pounds)
1 small onion, sliced
⅓ cup mango chutney (chop large pieces of mango, if necessary)
1 tablespoon lime juice
2 cloves garlic, minced
2 tablespoons cornstarch
2 tablespoons water
3 cups hot cooked linguini
Optional toppings: chopped cilantro, chopped peanuts or toasted coconut

Continental Chicken

1 package (2¼ ounces) dried beef, cut into pieces
4 boneless skinless chicken breasts (about 1 pound)
4 slices lean bacon
1 can (10¾ ounces) condensed cream of mushroom soup, undiluted
¼ cup all-purpose flour
¼ cup reduced-fat sour cream
Hot cooked noodles

1. Coat **CROCK-POT®** slow cooker with nonstick cooking spray. Place dried beef in bottom. Wrap each chicken breast with one bacon slice. Place wrapped chicken on top of dried beef.

2. Combine soup and flour in medium bowl until smooth. Pour over chicken. Cover; cook on LOW 7 to 8 hours or on HIGH 3 to 4 hours.

3. Place sour cream in small bowl; stir in a few tablespoons of cooking liquid from **CROCK-POT®** slow cooker. Stir sour cream mixture into remaining cooking liquid. Cook 5 minutes or until hot. Serve chicken and sauce over noodles.

Makes 4 servings

Creamy Chicken and Mushrooms

1. Combine salt, pepper and paprika in small bowl; sprinkle over chicken.

2. Layer chicken, mushrooms, green onions and bouillon in **CROCK-POT®** slow cooker. Pour wine and water over top. Cover; cook on HIGH 3 hours or on LOW 5 to 6 hours. Transfer chicken and vegetables to platter; cover with foil to keep warm.

3. Combine evaporated milk and cornstarch in small saucepan, stirring until smooth. Add 2 cups cooking liquid from **CROCK-POT®** slow cooker; bring to a boil. Boil 1 minute or until thickened, stirring constantly. Serve chicken and sauce over rice.

Makes 3 to 4 servings

1 teaspoon salt
½ teaspoon black pepper
¼ teaspoon paprika
3 boneless skinless chicken breasts, cut up
1½ cups sliced fresh mushrooms
½ cup sliced green onions
1¾ teaspoons chicken bouillon granules
1 cup dry white wine
½ cup water
1 can (5 ounces) evaporated milk
5 teaspoons cornstarch
Hot cooked rice

4 chicken legs
Salt and black pepper, to taste
2 tablespoons olive oil
½ pound fresh mushrooms, sliced
1 onion, sliced into rings
½ cup red wine
½ teaspoon dried basil
½ teaspoon dried thyme
½ teaspoon dried oregano
Hot cooked rice

Simple Coq au Vin

1. Sprinkle chicken with salt and pepper. Heat oil in large skillet over medium-high heat until hot. Brown chicken on both sides. Transfer chicken to **CROCK-POT**® slow cooker.

2. Add mushrooms and onion to skillet; cook and stir until onions are tender. Add wine; stir and scrape brown bits from bottom of skillet. Add mixture to **CROCK-POT**® slow cooker. Sprinkle with basil, thyme and oregano. Cover; cook on LOW 8 to 10 hours or on HIGH 3 to 4 hours.

3. Serve chicken and sauce over rice.

Makes 4 servings

Mu Shu Turkey

1. Place plums in blender or food processor. Cover; blend until almost smooth. Combine plums, orange juice, onion, ginger and cinnamon in **CROCK-POT®** slow cooker; mix well.

2. Place turkey over plum mixture. Cover; cook on LOW 3 to 4 hours.

3. Remove turkey from **CROCK-POT®** slow cooker. Divide evenly among tortillas. Spoon about 2 tablespoons plum sauce over turkey in each tortilla; top with about ½ cup coleslaw mix. Fold up bottom edge of tortilla over filling, fold in sides, and roll up to enclose filling. Repeat with remaining tortillas. Use remaining plum sauce for dipping.

Makes 6 servings

1 can (16 ounces) plums, drained and pitted
½ cup orange juice
¼ cup finely chopped onion
1 tablespoon minced fresh ginger
¼ teaspoon ground cinnamon
1 pound boneless turkey breast, cut into thin strips
6 (7-inch) flour tortillas
3 cups coleslaw mix

1 tablespoon olive oil
1 large onion, finely chopped
4 boneless skinless chicken thighs (about 1 pound), chopped
¼ pound smoked turkey sausage, finely chopped
3 cloves garlic, minced
1 teaspoon dried thyme
½ teaspoon black pepper
4 tablespoons tomato paste
2 tablespoons water
3 cans (about 15 ounces each) Great Northern beans, rinsed and drained
½ cup dry bread crumbs
3 tablespoons minced fresh parsley

Hearty Cassoulet

1. Heat oil in large skillet over medium heat until hot. Add onion. Cook and stir 5 minutes or until onion is tender. Stir in chicken, sausage, garlic, thyme and pepper. Cook 5 minutes or until chicken and sausage are browned.

2. Remove skillet from heat; stir in tomato paste and water until blended. Place beans and chicken mixture in **CROCK-POT**® slow cooker. Cover; cook on LOW 4 to 4½ hours.

3. Before serving, combine bread crumbs and parsley in small bowl. Sprinkle over top of cassoulet.

Makes 6 servings

Chili Verde

1. Coat large skillet with nonstick cooking spray. Heat over medium-high heat until hot. Add pork; cook until browned on all sides.

2. Combine pork and all remaining ingredients, except cilantro, in **CROCK-POT**® slow cooker. Cover; cook on HIGH 3 to 4 hours.

3. Season to taste with additional salt and pepper. Reduce heat to LOW. Stir in cilantro and cook 10 minutes.

Makes 4 servings

¾ pound boneless lean pork, cut into 1-inch cubes

1 can (15 ounces) Great Northern beans, rinsed and drained

1 can (14½ ounces) chicken broth

1 pound fresh tomatillos, husks removed, rinsed and coarsely chopped

1 large onion, halved and thinly sliced

1 can (4 ounces) diced mild green chilies

6 cloves garlic, chopped or sliced

1 teaspoon ground cumin
Salt and black pepper, to taste

½ cup lightly packed fresh cilantro, chopped

Parsnip and Carrot Soup

1. Coat small skillet with nonstick cooking spray. Heat over medium heat until hot. Add leek; cook and stir until golden. Transfer to **CROCK-POT®** slow cooker.

2. Add parsnips, carrots, broth, bay leaf, salt and pepper. Cover; cook on LOW 6 to 9 hours or on HIGH 2 to 4 hours, or until vegetables are tender.

3. Add pasta during last hour of cooking. Remove bay leaf before serving. To serve, sprinkle with croutons and parsley.

Makes 4 servings

Tip: For 5-, 6- or 7-quart **CROCK-POT®** slow cooker, double all ingredients.

1 medium leek, thinly sliced
4 medium parsnips, peeled and diced
4 medium carrots, peeled and diced
4 cups fat-free chicken broth
1 bay leaf
½ teaspoon salt
½ teaspoon black pepper
½ cup small pasta, cooked and drained
1 cup low-fat croutons
1 tablespoon chopped Italian parsley

Chicken and Sweet Potato Stew

4 boneless skinless chicken breasts, cut into bite-size pieces
2 medium sweet potatoes, peeled and cubed
2 medium Yukon Gold potatoes, peeled and cubed
2 medium carrots, peeled and cut into ½-inch slices
1 can (28 ounces) whole stewed tomatoes
1 teaspoon salt
1 teaspoon paprika
1 teaspoon celery seeds
½ teaspoon black pepper
⅛ teaspoon ground cinnamon
⅛ teaspoon ground nutmeg
1 cup chicken broth
¼ cup fresh basil, chopped

1. Combine chicken, potatoes, carrots, tomatoes, salt, paprika, celery seeds, pepper, cinnamon, nutmeg and broth in **CROCK-POT®** slow cooker.

2. Cover; cook on LOW 6 to 8 hours or on HIGH 3 to 4 hours.

3. To serve, sprinkle with basil.

Makes 6 servings

Tip: For 5-, 6- or 7-quart **CROCK-POT®** slow cooker, double all ingredients.

Bean and Corn Chili

1. Heat red wine and olive oil in medium skillet over medium heat until hot. Add onions and garlic; cook and stir until onions are tender. Transfer to **CROCK-POT**® slow cooker.

2. Add bell peppers, celery, tomatoes, beans, broth, tomato paste, corn, salt, chili powder, black pepper, cumin, red pepper, oregano and coriander. Mix well.

3. Cover; cook on LOW 6 to 8 hours or on HIGH 3 to 4 hours.

Makes 6 servings

Tip: For 5-, 6- or 7-quart **CROCK-POT**® slow cooker, double all ingredients.

2 tablespoons red wine
½ teaspoon olive oil
2 medium onions, finely chopped
5 cloves garlic, minced
1 green bell pepper, finely chopped
1 red bell pepper, finely chopped
1 rib celery, finely sliced
6 Roma or plum tomatoes, chopped
2 cans (15 ounces each) kidney beans, rinsed and drained
1½ cups fat-free chicken or vegetable broth
1 can (6 ounces) tomato paste
1 cup frozen corn kernels
1 teaspoon salt
1 teaspoon chili powder
½ teaspoon black pepper
¼ teaspoon cumin
¼ teaspoon ground red pepper
¼ teaspoon dried oregano
¼ teaspoon ground coriander

Savory Soups & Stews

Roast Tomato-Basil Soup

2 cans (28 ounces each) peeled whole tomatoes, drained and 3 cups liquid reserved
2½ tablespoons packed dark brown sugar
1 medium onion, finely chopped
3 cups chicken broth
3 tablespoons tomato paste
¼ teaspoon ground allspice
1 can (5 ounces) evaporated milk
¼ cup shredded fresh basil (about 10 large leaves)
Salt and black pepper, to taste

1. Preheat oven to 450°F. Line baking sheet with foil; spray with nonstick cooking spray. Arrange tomatoes on foil in single layer. Sprinkle with brown sugar and top with onion. Bake about 25 to 30 minutes or until tomatoes look dry and light brown. Let tomatoes cool slightly; finely chop.

2. Place tomato mixture, 3 cups reserved liquid from tomatoes, broth, tomato paste and allspice in **CROCK-POT**® slow cooker. Mix well. Cover; cook on LOW 8 hours or on HIGH 4 hours.

3. Add evaporated milk and basil; season with salt and pepper. Cook on HIGH 30 minutes or until hot.

Makes 6 servings

Simmering Hot and Sour Soup

1. Combine chicken broth, chicken, mushrooms, bamboo shoots, vinegar, soy sauce and chili paste in **CROCK-POT**® slow cooker. Cover; cook on LOW 3 to 4 hours or on HIGH 2 to 3 hours or until done.

2. Stir in tofu and sesame oil. Combine cornstarch with water; mix well. Add to soup and mix in well. Cover; cook on HIGH 10 minutes or until soup has thickened.

3. To serve, sprinkle with cilantro.

Makes 4 servings

2 cans (14½ ounces each) chicken broth
1 cup chopped cooked chicken or pork
4 ounces fresh shiitake mushroom caps, thinly sliced
½ cup sliced bamboo shoots, cut into thin strips
3 tablespoons rice wine vinegar
2 tablespoons soy sauce
1½ teaspoons chili paste *or* 1 teaspoon hot chili oil
4 ounces firm tofu, well drained and cut into ½-inch pieces
2 teaspoons sesame oil
2 tablespoons cornstarch
2 tablespoons cold water
Chopped cilantro *or* sliced green onions

Mama's Beer Chili

2 tablespoons olive oil
1 large onion (Vidalia if available), diced
4 cloves garlic, crushed
1½ to 2 pounds ground turkey
1 can (28 ounces) crushed tomatoes
1 cup beer (dark preferred)
3 tablespoons chili powder
1 teaspoon curry powder
3 tablespoons hot sauce
⅓ cup honey
1 package (10 ounces) frozen corn
1 can (15 ounces) pink beans or kidney beans
⅓ cup diced mild green chilies
3 beef bouillon cubes
1 to 2 tablespoons flour, to thicken

1. Heat oil in large skillet over medium-low heat until hot. Add onion; cook and stir 5 minutes. Add garlic; cook and stir 2 minutes.

2. Add turkey to skillet. Cook and stir until turkey is no longer pink. Drain fat and discard.

3. Add remaining ingredients, stirring until mixed. Transfer to **CROCK-POT®** slow cooker. Cover; cook on LOW 8 to 10 hours or on HIGH 4 to 6 hours.

Makes 4 to 6 servings

Chicken Stew with Herb Dumplings

1. Reserve 1 cup broth. Combine carrots, onion, bell pepper, celery and remaining broth in **CROCK-POT®** slow cooker. Cover; cook on LOW 2 hours.

2. Stir remaining 1 cup broth into flour until smooth. Stir into vegetable mixture. Add chicken, potato, mushrooms, peas, 1 teaspoon basil, ¾ teaspoon rosemary and ¼ teaspoon tarragon. Cover; cook on LOW 4 hours or until vegetables and chicken are tender. Stir in salt, pepper and cream.

3. Combine baking mix, ¼ teaspoon basil, ¼ teaspoon rosemary and ⅛ teaspoon tarragon in small bowl. Stir in milk to form soft dough. Add dumpling mixture to top of stew in 4 large spoonfuls. Cook, uncovered, 30 minutes. Cover; cook 30 to 45 minutes or until dumplings are firm and toothpick inserted in center comes out clean. Serve in shallow bowls.

Makes 4 servings

2 cans (14½ ounces each) chicken broth, divided
2 cups sliced carrots
1 cup chopped onion
1 large green bell pepper, sliced
½ cup sliced celery
⅔ cup all-purpose flour
1 pound boneless skinless chicken breasts, cut into 1-inch pieces
1 large red potato, unpeeled and cut into 1-inch pieces
6 ounces fresh mushrooms, halved
¾ cup frozen peas
1 teaspoon dried basil
¾ teaspoon dried rosemary
¼ teaspoon dried tarragon
¾ to 1 teaspoon salt
¼ teaspoon black pepper
¼ cup heavy cream

HERB DUMPLINGS
1 cup biscuit baking mix
¼ teaspoon dried basil
¼ teaspoon dried rosemary
⅛ teaspoon dried tarragon
⅓ cup reduced-fat (2%) milk

Beef Stew with Molasses and Raisins

⅓ cup all-purpose flour
2 teaspoons salt, divided
1½ teaspoons black pepper, divided
2 pounds beef for stew, cut into 1½-inch pieces
5 tablespoons oil, divided
2 medium onions, sliced
1 can (28 ounces) diced tomatoes, drained
1 cup beef broth
3 tablespoons molasses
2 tablespoons cider vinegar
4 cloves garlic, minced
2 teaspoons dried thyme
1 teaspoon celery salt
1 bay leaf
8 ounces baby carrots, cut in half lengthwise
2 parsnips, diced
½ cup golden raisins

1. Combine flour, 1½ teaspoons salt and 1 teaspoon pepper in large bowl. Toss meat in flour mixture. Heat 2 tablespoons oil in large skillet or Dutch oven over medium-high heat until hot. Add half of beef and brown on all sides. Set aside browned beef and repeat with 2 additional tablespoons oil and remaining beef.

2. Add remaining 1 tablespoon oil to skillet. Add onions and cook, stirring to loosen any browned bits, about 5 minutes. Add tomatoes, broth, molasses, vinegar, garlic, thyme, celery salt, bay leaf and remaining ½ teaspoon salt and ½ teaspoon pepper. Bring to a boil. Add browned beef and boil 1 minute.

3. Transfer mixture to **CROCK-POT®** slow cooker. Cover; cook on LOW 5 hours or on HIGH 2½ hours. Add carrots, parsnips and raisins. Cook 1 to 2 hours longer or until vegetables are tender. Remove and discard bay leaf.

Makes 6 to 8 servings

Golden Harvest Pork Stew

1. Toss pork pieces with 1 tablespoon flour; set aside. Heat oil in large skillet over medium-high heat until hot. Add pork; cook until browned on all sides. Transfer to **CROCK-POT**® slow cooker.

2. Add remaining ingredients, except parsley and 1 tablespoon flour. Cover; cook on LOW 5 to 6 hours.

3. Combine remaining 1 tablespoon flour and ¼ cup cooking liquid from stew in small bowl; stir until smooth. Stir flour mixture into stew. Cook on HIGH 10 minutes or until thickened. Adjust seasonings, if desired. To serve, sprinkle with parsley.

Makes 4 servings

- 1 pound boneless pork cutlets, cut into 1-inch pieces
- 2 tablespoons all-purpose flour, divided
- 1 tablespoon vegetable oil
- 2 medium Yukon Gold potatoes, unpeeled and cut into 1-inch cubes
- 1 large sweet potato, peeled and cut into 1-inch cubes
- 1 cup chopped carrots
- 1 ear corn, broken into 4 pieces *or* ½ cup corn
- ½ cup chicken broth
- 1 jalapeño pepper, seeded and finely chopped
- 1 clove garlic, minced
- 1 teaspoon salt
- ¼ teaspoon black pepper
- ¼ teaspoon dried thyme
  Chopped parsley

Mediterranean Stew

1 medium butternut squash, peeled and cut into 1-inch cubes
2 cups unpeeled eggplant, cut into 1-inch cubes
2 cups sliced zucchini
1 can (15½ ounces) chickpeas, rinsed and drained
1 package (10 ounces) frozen cut okra
1 can (8 ounces) tomato sauce
1 cup chopped onion
1 medium tomato, chopped
1 medium carrot, sliced
½ cup vegetable broth
⅓ cup raisins
1 clove garlic, minced
½ teaspoon ground cumin
½ teaspoon ground turmeric
¼ teaspoon ground red pepper
¼ teaspoon ground cinnamon
¼ teaspoon paprika
6 to 8 cups hot cooked couscous or rice

1. Combine all ingredients except couscous in **CROCK-POT®** slow cooker; mix well.

2. Cover; cook on LOW 8 to 10 hours or until vegetables are crisp-tender.

3. Serve over couscous. Garnish with parsley, if desired.

Makes 6 servings

Creamy Cauliflower Bisque

1. Combine cauliflower, potatoes, onion, broth, thyme, garlic powder and red pepper in **CROCK-POT®** slow cooker. Cover; cook on HIGH 4 hours or on LOW 8 hours.

2. Working in batches, place soup in blender and process until smooth, holding blender lid down firmly. Return to **CROCK-POT®** slow cooker. Add milk, butter, salt and black pepper. Stir until blended and warmed through.

3. To serve, top with cheese, parsley and green onions.

Makes 9 servings

1 pound frozen
   cauliflower florets
1 pound baking potatoes,
   peeled and cut in
   1-inch cubes
1 cup chopped onion
2 cans (14 ounces each)
   chicken broth
½ teaspoon dried thyme
¼ teaspoon garlic powder
⅛ teaspoon ground red
   pepper
1 cup evaporated milk
2 tablespoons butter
½ teaspoon salt
¼ teaspoon black pepper
1 cup shredded sharp
   Cheddar cheese
¼ cup finely chopped fresh
   parsley
¼ cup finely chopped
   green onions with top

2 cans (14 ounces each) chicken broth
1½ cups hot water
1 cup dried black beans, sorted and rinsed
1 cup chopped onion
2 bay leaves
1 teaspoon sugar
⅛ teaspoon ground red pepper
6 ounces reduced-fat country pork sausage
1 cup chopped tomato
1 tablespoon Worcestershire sauce
2 teaspoons extra-virgin olive oil
1 tablespoon chili powder
1½ teaspoons ground cumin
½ teaspoon salt
¼ cup chopped cilantro

Country Sausage and Bean Soup

1. Combine broth, water, beans, onions, bay leaves, sugar and red pepper in **CROCK-POT®** slow cooker. Cover; cook on LOW 8 hours or on HIGH 4 hours.

2. Coat large skillet with nonstick cooking spray. Heat over medium-high heat until hot. Add sausage and cook until beginning to brown, stirring to break up meat.

3. Add sausage and remaining ingredients, except cilantro, to **CROCK-POT®** slow cooker. Cover; cook on HIGH 15 minutes to blend flavors. To serve, sprinkle with cilantro.

Makes 9 servings

Beef Stew with Bacon, Onion and Sweet Potatoes

1. Coat **CROCK-POT**® slow cooker with nonstick cooking spray. Combine all ingredients, except cornstarch and water, in **CROCK-POT**® slow cooker; mix well. Cover; cook on LOW 7 to 8 hours or on HIGH 4 to 5 hours, or until meat and vegetables are tender.

2. With slotted spoon, transfer beef and vegetables to serving bowl; cover with foil to keep warm.

3. Turn **CROCK-POT**® slow cooker to HIGH. Combine cornstarch and water; stir until smooth. Stir into cooking liquid. Cover; cook 15 minutes or until thickened. To serve, spoon sauce over beef and vegetables.

Makes 4 servings

1 pound beef for stew, cut into 1-inch chunks
1 can (14½ ounces) beef broth
2 medium sweet potatoes, peeled and cut into 2-inch chunks
1 large onion, cut into 1½-inch chunks
2 slices thick-cut bacon, diced
1 teaspoon dried thyme
1 teaspoon salt
¼ teaspoon black pepper
2 tablespoons cornstarch
2 tablespoons water

Chicken and Black Bean Chili

1 pound boneless skinless chicken thighs, cut into 1-inch chunks
2 teaspoons chili powder
2 teaspoons ground cumin
¾ teaspoon salt
1 green bell pepper, diced
1 small onion, chopped
3 cloves garlic, minced
1 can (14½ ounces) diced tomatoes, undrained
1 cup chunky salsa
1 can (16 ounces) black beans, rinsed and drained
Toppings: sour cream, diced ripe avocado, shredded Cheddar cheese, sliced green onions or chopped cilantro, crushed tortilla or corn chips

1. Combine chicken, chili powder, cumin and salt in **CROCK-POT®** slow cooker, tossing to coat.

2. Add bell pepper, onion and garlic; mix well. Stir in tomatoes with juice and salsa. Cover; cook on LOW 5 to 6 hours or on HIGH 2½ to 3 hours, or until chicken is tender.

3. Turn **CROCK-POT®** slow cooker to HIGH; stir in beans. Cover; cook 5 to 10 minutes or until beans are heated through. Ladle into shallow bowls; serve with desired toppings.

Makes 4 servings

Beer and Cheese Soup

1. Preheat oven to 425°F. Slice bread into ½-inch cubes; place on baking sheet. Bake 10 to 12 minutes or until crisp, stirring once; set croutons aside.

2. Combine broth, beer, onion, garlic and thyme in **CROCK-POT®** slow cooker. Cover; cook on LOW 4 hours.

3. Turn **CROCK-POT®** slow cooker to HIGH. Stir in cheeses, milk and paprika. Cover; cook 45 minutes to 1 hour or until soup is hot and cheeses are melted. Stir soup well to blend cheeses. Ladle soup into bowls; top with croutons.

Makes 4 servings

Tip: For 5-, 6- or 7-quart **CROCK-POT®** slow cooker, double all ingredients.

2 to 3 slices pumpernickel or rye bread
1 can (14½ ounces) chicken broth
1 cup beer
¼ cup finely chopped onion
2 cloves garlic, minced
¾ teaspoon dried thyme
6 ounces American cheese, shredded or diced
4 to 6 ounces sharp Cheddar cheese, shredded
1 cup milk
½ teaspoon paprika

1½ pounds ground beef
1½ cups chopped onion
1 cup chopped green bell pepper
2 cloves garlic, minced
3 cans (15 ounces each) dark red kidney beans, rinsed and drained
2 cans (15 ounces each) tomato sauce
1 can (14½ ounces) diced tomatoes, undrained
2 to 3 teaspoons chili powder
1 to 2 teaspoons dry hot mustard
¾ teaspoon dried basil
½ teaspoon black pepper
1 to 2 dried hot chili peppers (optional)

Great Chili

1. Cook and stir ground beef, onion, bell pepper and garlic in large skillet until meat is browned and onion is tender. Drain fat and discard. Transfer mixture to 5-quart **CROCK-POT®** slow cooker.

2. Add beans, tomato sauce, tomatoes with juice, chili powder, mustard, basil, black pepper and chili peppers, if desired; mix well. Cover; cook on LOW 8 to 10 hours or on HIGH 4 to 5 hours.

3. If used, remove chili peppers before serving.

Makes 6 servings

Potato & Spinach Soup with Gouda

1. Combine potatoes, broth, water, onion, spinach, salt and red and black pepper in **CROCK-POT®** slow cooker. Cover; cook on LOW 10 hours or until potatoes are tender.

2. Slightly mash potatoes in **CROCK-POT®** slow cooker; add 2 cups Gouda and evaporated milk. Cover; cook on HIGH 15 to 20 minutes or until cheese is melted.

3. Heat oil in small skillet over low heat until hot. Cook and stir garlic until golden brown; set aside. Pour soup into bowls. Sprinkle 2 to 3 teaspoons remaining Gouda cheese in each bowl. Place spoonful of garlic in center of each bowl; sprinkle with parsley.

Makes 8 to 10 servings

9 medium Yukon Gold potatoes, peeled and cubed (about 6 cups)
2 cans (14 ounces each) chicken broth
½ cup water
1 small red onion, finely chopped
5 ounces baby spinach
½ teaspoon salt
¼ teaspoon ground red pepper
¼ teaspoon black pepper
2½ cups shredded smoked Gouda cheese, divided
1 can (12 ounces) evaporated milk
1 tablespoon olive oil
4 cloves garlic, cut into thin slices
5 to 7 sprigs parsley, finely chopped

1 cup diced red potatoes
1 cup coarsely chopped carrots
2 cans (14½ ounces each) beef broth
1 can (14½ ounces) diced tomatoes, undrained
1 cup coarsely chopped green cabbage
1 cup sliced zucchini
¾ cup chopped onion
¾ cup sliced fresh green beans
¾ cup coarsely chopped celery
¾ cup water
2 tablespoons olive oil
1 clove garlic, minced
½ teaspoon dried basil
¼ teaspoon dried rosemary
1 bay leaf
1 can (15 ounces) cannellini beans, rinsed and drained
Shredded Parmesan cheese (optional)

Minestrone alla Milanese

1. Combine all ingredients except cannellini beans and cheese in **CROCK-POT®** slow cooker; mix well. Cover; cook on LOW 5 to 6 hours.

2. Add cannellini beans. Cover; cook on LOW 1 hour or until vegetables are tender.

3. Remove and discard bay leaf. Garnish with cheese, if desired.

Makes 8 to 10 servings

Vegetarian Chili

1. Heat oil in large skillet over medium-high heat until hot. Add onion, bell pepper, jalapeño pepper and garlic; cook and stir 5 minutes or until vegetables are tender. Transfer vegetables to **CROCK-POT**® slow cooker.

2. Add remaining ingredients except sour cream and cheese; mix well. Cover; cook on LOW 4 to 5 hours.

3. Garnish with sour cream and cheese, if desired.

Makes 4 servings

1 tablespoon vegetable oil
1 cup chopped onion
1 cup chopped red bell pepper
2 tablespoons minced jalapeño pepper
1 clove garlic, minced
1 can (28 ounces) crushed tomatoes
1 can (15 ounces) black beans, rinsed and drained
1 can (15 ounces) chickpeas, rinsed and drained
½ cup corn
¼ cup tomato paste
1 teaspoon sugar
1 teaspoon ground cumin
1 teaspoon dried basil
1 teaspoon chili powder
¼ teaspoon black pepper
Sour cream and shredded Cheddar cheese (optional)

Hearty Veggies & Sides

Spinach Spoon Bread

1 package (10 ounces)
    frozen chopped
    spinach, thawed and
    squeezed dry
1 red bell pepper, diced
4 eggs, lightly beaten
1 cup cottage cheese
1 package (5½ ounces)
    cornbread mix
6 green onions, sliced
½ cup (1 stick) butter,
    melted
1¼ teaspoons seasoned salt

1. Coat **CROCK-POT**® slow cooker with nonstick cooking spray; preheat on HIGH.

2. Combine all ingredients in large bowl; mix well. Pour batter into prepared **CROCK-POT**® slow cooker. Cook, covered, with lid slightly ajar to allow excess moisture to escape, on LOW 3 to 4 hours or on HIGH 1¾ to 2 hours, or until edges are golden and knife inserted in center of bread comes out clean.

3. Loosen edges and bottom with knife and invert onto plate. Cut into wedges to serve. Or, serve bread spooned from **CROCK-POT**® slow cooker.

Makes 8 servings

Winter Squash and Apples

1 teaspoon salt
½ teaspoon black pepper
1 butternut squash (about 2 pounds), peeled and seeded
2 apples, cored and cut into slices
1 medium onion, quartered and sliced
1½ tablespoons butter

1. Combine salt and pepper in small bowl; set aside.

2. Cut squash into 2-inch pieces; place in **CROCK-POT**® slow cooker. Add apples and onion. Sprinkle with salt mixture; stir well. Cover; cook on LOW 6 to 7 hours or until vegetables are tender.

3. Just before serving, stir in butter and season to taste with additional salt and pepper.

Makes 4 to 6 servings

Spanish Paella-Style Rice

1. Combine broth, rice, bell pepper, wine, saffron and pepper flakes in **CROCK-POT®** slow cooker; mix well.

2. Cover; cook on LOW 4 hours or until liquid is absorbed.

3. Stir in peas. Cover; cook 15 to 30 minutes or until peas are hot. Season with salt.

Makes 6 servings

2 cans (14½ ounces each) chicken broth
1½ cups uncooked converted long-grain rice
1 small red bell pepper, diced
⅓ cup dry white wine or water
½ teaspoon saffron threads, crushed *or* ½ teaspoon ground turmeric
⅛ teaspoon red pepper flakes
½ cup frozen peas, thawed
Salt, to taste

Hearty Veggies & Sides

Scalloped Potatoes and Parsnips

6 tablespoons unsalted butter

3 tablespoons all-purpose flour

1¾ cups whipping cream

2 teaspoons dry mustard

1½ teaspoons salt

1 teaspoon dried thyme

½ teaspoon black pepper

2 baking potatoes, cut in half lengthwise, then crosswise into ¼-inch slices

2 parsnips, cut into ¼-inch slices

1 onion, chopped

2 cups (8 ounces) shredded sharp Cheddar cheese

1. To prepare cream sauce, melt butter in medium saucepan over medium-high heat. Whisk in flour; cook 1 to 2 minutes. Slowly whisk in cream, mustard, salt, thyme and pepper until smooth.

2. Place potatoes, parsnips and onion in **CROCK-POT®** slow cooker. Add cream sauce. Cover; cook on LOW 7 hours or on HIGH 3½ hours or until potatoes are tender.

3. Stir in cheese. Cover; let stand until cheese melts.

Makes 4 to 6 servings

Southwestern Stuffed Peppers

1. Cut thin slice off top of each bell pepper. Carefully remove seeds, leaving pepper whole.

2. Combine beans, cheese, salsa, corn, onions, rice, chili powder and cumin in medium bowl. Spoon filling evenly into each pepper. Place peppers in **CROCK-POT®** slow cooker.

3. Cover; cook on LOW 4 to 6 hours. Serve with sour cream, if desired.

Makes 4 servings

4 green bell peppers
1 can (15 ounces) black beans, rinsed and drained
1 cup (4 ounces) shredded pepper-jack cheese
¾ cup medium salsa
½ cup frozen corn, thawed
½ cup chopped green onions with tops
⅓ cup uncooked long-grain white rice
1 teaspoon chili powder
½ teaspoon ground cumin
Sour cream (optional)

Deluxe Potato Casserole

1 can (10¾ ounces) condensed cream of chicken soup

1 cup (8 ounces) sour cream

¼ cup chopped onion

¼ cup plus 3 tablespoons melted butter, divided

1 teaspoon salt

2 pounds red potatoes, peeled and chopped

2 cups (8 ounces) shredded Cheddar cheese

1½ to 2 cups stuffing mix

1. Combine soup, sour cream, onion, ¼ cup butter and salt in small bowl.

2. Combine potatoes and cheese in **CROCK-POT®** slow cooker. Pour soup mixture over potato mixture; mix well.

3. Sprinkle stuffing mix over potato mixture; drizzle with remaining 3 tablespoons butter. Cover; cook on LOW 8 to 10 hours or on HIGH 5 to 6 hours, or until potatoes are tender.

Makes 8 to 10 servings

Herbed Fall Vegetables

1. Combine potatoes, parsnips, fennel, herbs and butter in **CROCK-POT**® slow cooker.

2. Whisk together broth, mustard, salt and pepper in small bowl. Pour mixture over vegetables.

3. Cover; cook on LOW 4½ hours or on HIGH 3 hours, or until vegetables are tender, stirring occasionally to ensure even cooking.

Makes 6 servings

2 medium Yukon Gold potatoes, peeled and cut into ½-inch dice
2 medium sweet potatoes, peeled and cut into ½-inch dice
3 parsnips, peeled and cut into ½-inch dice
1 medium head fennel, sliced and cut into ½-inch dice
½ to ¾ cup chopped fresh herbs, such as tarragon, parsley, sage or thyme
¼ cup (½ stick) butter, cut into small pieces
1 cup chicken broth
1 tablespoon Dijon mustard
1 tablespoon salt
Black pepper, to taste

Chicken Broth

Dijon Mustard

Mama's Best Baked Beans

1 bag (1 pound) dried Great Northern beans
1 package (1 pound) bacon
5 hot dogs, cut into ½-inch pieces
1 cup chopped onion
1 bottle (24 ounces) ketchup
2 cups packed dark brown sugar

1. Soak and cook beans according to package directions. Drain and refrigerate until ready to use.

2. Cook bacon in large skillet over medium-high heat until crisp. Transfer to paper towels to drain. Cool, then crumble bacon; set aside. Discard all but 3 tablespoons bacon fat from skillet. Add hot dogs and onion. Cook and stir over medium heat until onion is tender.

3. Combine cooked beans, bacon, hot dog mixture, ketchup and brown sugar in **CROCK-POT®** slow cooker. Cover; cook on LOW 2 to 4 hours.

Makes 4 to 6 servings

Cheesy Broccoli Casserole

1. Coat **CROCK-POT®** slow cooker with nonstick cooking spray. Combine broccoli, soup, 1 cup cheese, onions, celery seed, paprika and hot sauce in **CROCK-POT®** slow cooker; mix well.

2. Cover; cook on LOW 5 to 6 hours or on HIGH 2½ to 3 hours, or until done.

3. Uncover; sprinkle top with potato chips and remaining ¼ cup cheese. Cook, uncovered, on LOW 30 to 60 minutes or on HIGH 15 to 30 minutes, or until cheese melts.

Makes 4 to 6 servings

2 packages (10 ounces each) chopped broccoli, thawed
1 can (10¾ ounces) condensed cream of celery soup
1¼ cups shredded sharp Cheddar cheese, divided
¼ cup minced onions
½ teaspoon celery seed
1 teaspoon paprika
1 teaspoon hot pepper sauce
1 cup crushed potato chips or saltine crackers

Corn on the Cob with Garlic Herb Butter

½ cup (1 stick) unsalted butter, at room temperature

3 to 4 cloves garlic, minced

2 tablespoons finely minced fresh parsley

4 to 5 ears of corn, husked

Salt and black pepper, to taste

1. Thoroughly mix butter, garlic and parsley in small bowl.

2. Place each ear of corn on a piece of aluminum foil and generously spread butter on each ear. Season corn with salt and pepper and tightly seal foil.

3. Place corn in **CROCK-POT®** slow cooker; it's okay to overlap ears. Add enough water to come ¼ of the way up each ear. Cover; cook on LOW 4 to 5 hours or on HIGH 2 to 2½ hours or until done.

Makes 4 to 5 servings

Vegetarian Sausage Rice

1. Combine bell peppers, beans, tomatoes with juice, onion, celery, ½ cup water, rice, salt, hot sauce, thyme, pepper flakes and bay leaves in **CROCK-POT**® slow cooker. Cover; cook on LOW 4 to 5 hours. Remove and discard bay leaves.

2. Dice breakfast patties. Heat oil in large nonstick skillet over medium-high heat until hot. Add patties; cook 2 minutes or until lightly browned, scraping bottom of skillet occasionally.

3. Place patties in **CROCK-POT**® slow cooker. Do not stir. Add remaining ½ cup water to skillet; bring to a boil over high heat 1 minute, scraping up browned bits on bottom of skillet. Add liquid and parsley to **CROCK-POT**® slow cooker; stir gently to blend. Serve immediately with additional hot sauce, if desired.

Makes 8 cups

2 cups chopped green bell peppers
1 can (15 ounces) dark kidney beans, drained and rinsed
1 can (14½ ounces) diced tomatoes with green bell peppers and onions, undrained
1 cup chopped onion
1 cup sliced celery
1 cup water, divided
¾ cup uncooked converted long-grain rice
1¼ teaspoons salt
1 teaspoon hot pepper sauce
½ teaspoon dried thyme
½ teaspoon red pepper flakes
3 bay leaves
1 package (8 ounces) vegetable-protein breakfast patties, thawed
2 tablespoons extra-virgin olive oil
½ cup chopped fresh parsley
Additional hot pepper sauce (optional)

FILLING

- 1 medium onion, chopped
- 1 medium green bell pepper, diced
- 2 cloves garlic, minced
- 1 can (16 ounces) red kidney beans, rinsed and drained
- 1 can (16 ounces) pinto beans, rinsed and drained
- 1 can (16 ounces) diced tomatoes with jalapeño peppers, undrained
- 1 can (8 ounces) tomato sauce
- 1 teaspoon chili powder
- ½ teaspoon ground cumin
- ½ teaspoon black pepper
- ¼ teaspoon hot pepper sauce

TOPPING

- 1 cup yellow cornmeal
- 1 cup all-purpose flour
- 2½ teaspoons baking powder
- 1 tablespoon sugar
- ½ teaspoon salt
- 1¼ cups milk
- 2 eggs
- 3 tablespoons vegetable oil
- 1 can (8½ ounces) cream-style corn, undrained

Cornbread and Bean Casserole

1. Spray **CROCK-POT®** slow cooker with nonstick cooking spray. Cook onion, bell pepper and garlic in large skillet over medium heat until tender. Transfer to **CROCK-POT®** slow cooker.

2. Stir in beans, tomatoes with juice, tomato sauce, chili powder, cumin, black pepper and hot sauce. Cover; cook on HIGH 1 hour.

3. Combine cornmeal, flour, baking powder, sugar and salt in large bowl. Stir in milk, eggs and oil; mix well. Stir in corn. Spoon evenly over bean mixture in **CROCK-POT®** slow cooker. Cover; cook on HIGH 1½ to 2 hours or until cornbread topping is done.

Makes 6 to 8 servings

Tip: Spoon any remaining cornbread topping into greased muffin cups; bake 30 minutes at 375°F or until golden brown.

Broccoli and Cheese Strata

1. Butter 1-quart casserole or soufflé dish that will fit in **CROCK-POT**® slow cooker. Cook broccoli in boiling water 10 minutes or until tender. Drain. Spread one side of each bread slice with 1 teaspoon butter. Arrange 2 slices bread, buttered sides up, in prepared casserole dish. Layer cheese, broccoli and remaining 2 bread slices, buttered sides down.

2. Beat milk, eggs, salt, hot sauce and black pepper in medium bowl. Slowly pour over bread.

3. Place small wire rack in 5-quart **CROCK-POT**® slow cooker. Pour in 1 cup water. Place casserole on rack. Cover; cook on HIGH 3 hours.

Makes 4 servings

2 cups chopped broccoli florets
4 slices firm white bread, ½ inch thick
4 teaspoons butter
1½ cups (6 ounces) shredded Cheddar cheese
1½ cups low-fat (1%) milk
3 eggs
½ teaspoon salt
½ teaspoon hot pepper sauce
⅛ teaspoon black pepper

Risotto-Style Peppered Rice

1 cup uncooked converted long-grain rice
1 medium green bell pepper, chopped
1 medium red bell pepper, chopped
1 cup chopped onion
½ teaspoon ground turmeric
⅛ teaspoon ground red pepper (optional)
1 can (14½ ounces) fat-free chicken broth
4 ounces Monterey Jack cheese with jalapeño peppers, cubed
½ cup milk
¼ cup (½ stick) butter, cubed
1 teaspoon salt

1. Place rice, bell peppers, onion, turmeric and ground red pepper, if desired, in **CROCK-POT**® slow cooker. Stir in broth.

2. Cover; cook on LOW 4 to 5 hours or until rice is tender and broth is absorbed.

3. Stir in cheese, milk, butter and salt; fluff rice with fork. Cover; cook on LOW 5 minutes or until cheese melts.

Makes 4 to 6 servings

Spicy Beans Tex-Mex

1. Combine lentils and water in large saucepan. Boil 20 to 30 minutes; drain.

2. Cook bacon in medium skillet until crisp. Transfer to paper towels to drain. Cool, then crumble bacon. In same skillet, cook onion in bacon drippings until tender.

3. Combine lentils, bacon, onion, beans, tomatoes with juice, ketchup, garlic, chili powder, cumin, pepper flakes and bay leaf in **CROCK-POT®** slow cooker. Cover; cook on LOW 5 to 6 hours or on HIGH 3 to 4 hours. Remove bay leaf before serving.

Makes 8 to 10 servings

⅓ cup lentils
1⅓ cups water
5 strips bacon
1 onion, chopped
1 can (15 ounces) pinto beans, rinsed and drained
1 can (15 ounces) red kidney beans, rinsed and drained
1 can (14½ ounces) diced tomatoes, undrained
3 tablespoons ketchup
3 cloves garlic, minced
1 teaspoon chili powder
½ teaspoon ground cumin
¼ teaspoon red pepper flakes
1 bay leaf

Hearty Veggies & Sides

Jim's Mexican-Style Spinach

3 packages (10 ounces each) frozen chopped spinach
1 tablespoon canola oil
1 onion, chopped
1 clove garlic, minced
2 Anaheim chilies, roasted*, peeled and minced
3 fresh tomatillos, roasted**, husks removed and chopped
6 tablespoons fat-free sour cream (optional)

*To roast chilies, heat heavy frying pan over medium-high heat until drop of water sizzles. Cook chilies, turning occasionally with tongs, until blackened all over. Place chilies in brown paper bag for 2 to 5 minutes. Remove chilies from bag and scrape off charred skin. Cut off top with seed core. Cut lengthwise into halves. With a knife tip, scrape out veins and any remaining seeds.

*To roast fresh tomatillos, heat heavy frying pan over medium heat. Leaving papery husks on, cook tomatillos, turning often, until husks are brown and interior flesh is soft, about 10 minutes. When cool enough to handle, remove and discard husks.

1. Place frozen spinach in **CROCK-POT**® slow cooker.

2. Heat oil in large skillet over medium heat until hot. Cook and stir onion and garlic until onion is soft but not browned, about 5 minutes. Add chilies and tomatillos; cook 3 to 4 minutes longer. Add mixture to **CROCK-POT**® slow cooker.

3. Cover; cook on LOW 4 to 6 hours. Stir before serving. Serve with dollops of sour cream, if desired.

Makes 6 servings

Swiss Cheese Scalloped Potatoes

1. Layer half the potatoes, ¼ cup onion, ⅛ teaspoon salt, ⅛ teaspoon nutmeg and 1 tablespoon butter in **CROCK-POT®** slow cooker. Repeat layers. Cover; cook on LOW 7 hours or on HIGH 4 hours.

2. Remove potatoes with slotted spoon to serving dish and cover with foil to keep warm.

3. Blend milk and flour in small bowl until smooth. Stir mixture into cooking liquid. Add cheese; stir to combine. Turn **CROCK-POT®** slow cooker to HIGH. Cover; cook until slightly thickened, about 10 minutes. Stir, then pour cheese mixture over potatoes. To serve, garnish with chopped green onions, if desired.

Makes 5 to 6 servings

2 pounds baking potatoes, peeled and thinly sliced, divided
½ cup finely chopped yellow onion, divided
¼ teaspoon salt, divided
¼ teaspoon ground nutmeg, divided
2 tablespoons butter, cut into small pieces, divided
½ cup milk
2 tablespoons all-purpose flour
3 ounces Swiss cheese slices, torn into small pieces
¼ cup chopped green onions (optional)

Hearty Veggies & Sides

Orange-Spice Glazed Carrots

1 package (32 ounces) baby carrots
½ cup packed light brown sugar
½ cup orange juice
3 tablespoons butter or margarine
¾ teaspoon ground cinnamon
¼ teaspoon ground nutmeg
¼ cup cold water
2 tablespoons cornstarch

1. Combine carrots, sugar, orange juice, butter, cinnamon and nutmeg in **CROCK-POT®** slow cooker. Cover; cook on LOW 3½ to 4 hours or until carrots are crisp-tender.

2. Spoon carrots into serving bowl. Transfer cooking liquid to small saucepan. Bring to a boil.

3. Mix water and cornstarch until smooth; stir into saucepan. Boil 1 minute or until thickened, stirring constantly. Spoon over carrots.

Makes 6 servings

Pesto Rice and Beans

1. Combine beans, broth and rice in **CROCK-POT**® slow cooker. Cover; cook on LOW 2 hours.

2. Stir in green beans. Cover; cook 1 hour or until rice and beans are tender.

3. Turn off **CROCK-POT**® slow cooker and transfer stoneware to heatproof surface. Stir in pesto and Parmesan cheese, if desired. Let stand, covered, 5 minutes or until cheese is melted. Serve immediately.

Makes 8 servings

1 can (15 ounces) Great Northern beans, rinsed and drained
1 can (14 ounces) chicken broth
¾ cup uncooked converted long-grain rice
1½ cups frozen cut green beans, thawed and drained
½ cup prepared pesto
Grated Parmesan cheese (optional)

Bean and Vegetable Burritos

2 tablespoons chili powder
2 teaspoons dried oregano
1½ teaspoons ground cumin
1 large sweet potato, peeled and diced
1 can (15 ounces) black beans, rinsed and drained
4 cloves garlic, minced
1 medium onion, halved and thinly sliced
1 jalapeño pepper, seeded and minced
1 green bell pepper, chopped
1 cup frozen corn, thawed and drained
3 tablespoons lime juice
1 tablespoon chopped fresh cilantro
¾ cup (3 ounces) shredded Monterey Jack cheese
4 (10-inch) flour tortillas

1. Combine chili powder, oregano and cumin in small bowl. Set aside.

2. Layer ingredients in **CROCK-POT**® slow cooker in following order: sweet potato, beans, half of chili powder mixture, garlic, onion, jalapeño pepper, bell pepper, remaining half of chili powder mixture and corn. Cover; cook on LOW 5 hours or until sweet potato is tender. Stir in lime juice and cilantro.

3. Preheat oven to 350°F. Spoon 2 tablespoons cheese into center of each tortilla. Top with 1 cup filling. Fold up bottom edge of tortilla over filling, fold in sides and roll to enclose filling. Place burrito, seam side down, on baking sheet. Repeat with remaining tortillas. Cover with foil and bake 20 to 30 minutes or until heated through.

Makes 4 servings

Skinny Cornbread

1. Coat **CROCK-POT®** slow cooker with nonstick cooking spray.

2. Sift together flour, cornmeal, sugar, baking powder, baking soda and seasoned salt in large bowl. Make well in center of dry mixture. Pour in buttermilk, egg substitute and oil. Mix in dry ingredients just until moistened. Pour mixture into **CROCK-POT®** slow cooker.

3. Cook, covered, with lid slightly ajar to allow excess moisture to escape, on LOW 3 to 4 hours or on HIGH 45 minutes to 1½ hours, or until edges are golden and knife inserted into center comes out clean. Remove stoneware from **CROCK-POT®** slow cooker. Cool on wire rack about 10 minutes; remove bread from stoneware and cool completely on rack.

Makes 8 servings

Tip: This recipe works best in round **CROCK-POT®** slow cookers.

1¼ cups all-purpose flour
¾ cup yellow cornmeal
¼ cup sugar
1 teaspoon baking powder
1 teaspoon baking soda
1 teaspoon seasoned salt
1 cup fat-free buttermilk
¼ cup cholesterol-free egg substitute
¼ cup canola oil

Slow-Cooked Sweets

Brownie Bottoms

½ cup packed brown sugar
¾ cup water
2 tablespoons unsweetened cocoa powder
2½ cups packaged brownie mix
1 package (2¾ ounces) instant chocolate pudding mix
½ cup milk chocolate chips
2 eggs, beaten
3 tablespoons butter or margarine, melted

1. Lightly coat **CROCK-POT®** slow cooker with nonstick cooking spray. Combine brown sugar, water and cocoa powder in small saucepan; bring to a boil.

2. Combine brownie mix, pudding mix, chocolate chips, eggs and butter in medium bowl; stir until well blended. Spread batter into **CROCK-POT®** slow cooker. Pour boiling sugar mixture over batter. Cover; cook on HIGH 1½ hours.

3. Turn off **CROCK-POT®** slow cooker and let stand for 30 minutes. Serve warm with whipped cream or ice cream, if desired.

Makes 6 servings

Tip: For 5-, 6- or 7-quart **CROCK-POT®** slow cooker, double all ingredients.

**6 cups cooking apples,
peeled, cored and cut
into eighths**
1 cup bread crumbs
**1 teaspoon ground
cinnamon**
**1 teaspoon ground
nutmeg**
⅛ teaspoon salt
¾ cup packed brown sugar
**½ cup (1 stick) butter or
margarine, melted**
**¼ cup finely chopped
walnuts**

Homestyle Apple Brown Betty

1. Lightly grease **CROCK-POT®** slow cooker. Place apples in bottom.

2. Combine bread crumbs, cinnamon, nutmeg, salt, brown sugar, butter and walnuts. Spread over apples.

3. Cover; cook on LOW 3 to 4 hours or on HIGH 2 hours.

Makes 8 servings

Tip: For 5-, 6- or 7-quart **CROCK-POT®** slow cooker, double all ingredients.

Banana Nut Bread

1. Grease and flour **CROCK-POT®** slow cooker. Sift together flour, baking powder, salt and baking soda in small bowl; set aside.

2. Cream butter in large bowl with electric mixer until fluffy. Slowly add sugar, eggs, corn syrup and mashed bananas. Beat until smooth. Gradually add flour mixture to creamed mixture. Add walnuts and mix well. Pour into **CROCK-POT®** slow cooker. Cover; cook on HIGH 2 to 3 hours or until toothpick inserted into center comes out clean.

3. Let cool, then turn bread out onto serving platter.

Makes 6 servings

Tip: For 5-, 6- or 7-quart **CROCK-POT®** slow cooker, double all ingredients.

1¾ cups all-purpose flour
2 teaspoons baking powder
½ teaspoon salt
¼ teaspoon baking soda
⅓ cup butter or margarine
⅔ cup sugar
2 eggs, well beaten
2 tablespoons dark corn syrup
3 ripe bananas, well mashed
½ cup chopped walnuts

Mixed Berry Cobbler

1 package (16 ounces) frozen mixed berries
¾ cup granulated sugar
2 tablespoons quick-cooking tapioca
2 teaspoons grated lemon peel
1½ cups all-purpose flour
½ cup packed brown sugar
2¼ teaspoons baking powder
¼ teaspoon ground nutmeg
¾ cup milk
⅓ cup butter, melted
Vanilla ice cream (optional)

1. Stir together berries, granulated sugar, tapioca and lemon peel in **CROCK-POT®** slow cooker.

2. Combine flour, brown sugar, baking powder and nutmeg in medium bowl. Add milk and butter; stir just until blended. Drop spoonfuls of dough on top of berry mixture.

3. Cover; cook on LOW 4 hours. Uncover; let stand about 30 minutes. Serve with ice cream, if desired.

Makes 8 servings

Apple-Date Crisp

1. Coat **CROCK-POT**® slow cooker with nonstick cooking spray. Place apples in medium bowl. Sprinkle with lemon juice; toss to coat. Add dates and mix well. Transfer mixture to **CROCK-POT**® slow cooker.

2. Combine oats, flour, sugar, cinnamon, ginger, salt, nutmeg and cloves, if desired, in medium bowl. Cut in butter with pastry blender or two knives until mixture resembles coarse crumbs.

3. Sprinkle oat mixture over apples; smooth top. Cover; cook on LOW about 4 hours or on HIGH about 2 hours, or until apples are tender.

Makes 6 servings

6 cups thinly sliced peeled apples (about 6 medium apples, preferably Golden Delicious)
2 teaspoons lemon juice
⅓ cup chopped dates
1⅓ cups uncooked quick oats
½ cup all-purpose flour
½ cup packed light brown sugar
½ teaspoon ground cinnamon
¼ teaspoon ground ginger
¼ teaspoon salt
Dash ground nutmeg
Dash ground cloves (optional)
¼ cup (½ stick) cold butter, cut into small pieces

Coconut Rice Pudding

2 cups water
1 cup uncooked converted long-grain rice
1 tablespoon unsalted butter
Pinch salt
2¼ cups evaporated milk
1 can (14 ounces) cream of coconut
½ cup golden raisins
3 egg yolks, beaten
Grated peel of 2 limes
1 teaspoon vanilla
Toasted shredded coconut (optional)

1. Place water, rice, butter and salt in medium saucepan. Bring to a boil over high heat, stirring frequently. Reduce heat to low. Cover; cook 10 to 12 minutes. Remove from heat. Let stand, covered, 5 minutes.

2. Meanwhile, coat **CROCK-POT**® slow cooker with nonstick cooking spray. Add evaporated milk, cream of coconut, raisins, egg yolks, lime peel and vanilla; mix well. Add rice; stir until blended.

3. Cover; cook on LOW 4 hours or on HIGH 2 hours. Stir every 30 minutes, if possible. Pudding will thicken as it cools. Garnish with toasted shredded coconut, if desired.

Makes 6 servings

Cran-Apple Orange Conserve

1. Remove thin slice from both ends of both oranges for easier chopping. Finely chop unpeeled oranges and remove any seeds to yield about 2 cups of chopped oranges.

2. Combine chopped oranges, apples, sugar, cranberries and lemon peel in **CROCK-POT®** slow cooker. Cover; cook on LOW 4 hours or on HIGH 2 hours.

3. Slightly crush fruit with potato masher. Cook, uncovered, on LOW 2 hours or on HIGH 1 to 1½ hours or until very thick, stirring occasionally to prevent sticking. Cool at least 2 hours. Serve over pound cake, waffles or pancakes.

Makes about 5 cups

2 medium oranges, washed
5 large tart apples, peeled, cored and chopped
2 cups sugar
1½ cups fresh cranberries
1 tablespoon grated lemon peel
Pound cake

Fruit Ambrosia with Dumplings

4 cups fresh or frozen fruit*

½ cup granulated sugar, plus 2 tablespoons, divided

½ cup warm apple or cran-apple juice

2 tablespoons quick-cooking tapioca

1 cup all-purpose flour

1¼ teaspoons baking powder

¼ teaspoon salt

3 tablespoons butter, cut into small pieces

½ cup milk

1 large egg

2 tablespoons light brown sugar, plus additional for garnish

*Use strawberries, raspberries, blueberries or peaches.

1. Combine fruit, ½ cup granulated sugar, juice and tapioca in **CROCK-POT®** slow cooker. Cover; cook on LOW 5 to 6 hours or on HIGH 2½ to 3 hours, or until fruit forms thick sauce.

2. Combine flour, 2 tablespoons granulated sugar, baking powder, and salt in mixing bowl. Cut in butter using pastry cutter or two knives until the mixture resembles coarse crumbs. Stir together milk and egg in separate small bowl. Pour milk and egg mixture into flour mixture. Stir until soft dough forms. Turn **CROCK-POT®** slow cooker to HIGH. Drop dough by teaspoonfuls on top of fruit. Sprinkle dumplings with brown sugar. Cover; cook 30 minutes to 1 hour or until toothpick inserted in dumplings comes out clean.

3. Sprinkle dumplings with additional brown sugar, if desired. Serve warm with scoops of ice cream, sweetened whipped cream or fruity yogurt, if desired.

Makes 4 to 6 servings

Fresh Berry Compote

1. Place blueberries in **CROCK-POT®** slow cooker. Cover; cook on HIGH 45 minutes, until blueberries begin to soften.

2. Add strawberries, orange juice, ½ cup sugar, lemon peel and cinnamon stick. Stir to blend. Cover; cook 1 to 1½ hours, or until berries soften and sugar dissolves. Check for sweetness and add more sugar if necessary, cooking until added sugar dissolves.

3. Transfer **CROCK-POT®** stoneware insert from heating unit to heatproof surface to cool. Serve compote warm or chilled.

Makes 4 servings

2 cups fresh blueberries
4 cups fresh sliced strawberries
2 tablespoons orange juice
½ to ¾ cup sugar
4 slices (½ inch×1½ inch) lemon peel with no white pith
1 cinnamon stick *or* ½ teaspoon ground cinnamon

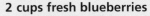

Berry Bread Pudding

6 cups bread, preferably dense peasant-style or sourdough, cut into ¾- to 1-inch cubes

½ cup slivered almonds, toasted

1 cup raisins

6 large eggs, beaten

1¾ cups milk (1% or greater)

1 teaspoon vanilla

2 cups packed brown sugar

1½ teaspoons ground cinnamon

3 cups sliced fresh strawberries

2 cups fresh blueberries

Fresh mint leaves (optional)

1. Coat **CROCK-POT**® slow cooker with nonstick cooking spray or butter. Place bread, nuts and raisins in bottom and toss to combine.

2. Whisk together eggs, milk, vanilla, sugar and cinnamon in separate bowl. Pour egg mixture over bread mixture; toss to blend. Cover; cook on LOW 4 to 4½ hours or on HIGH 3 hours.

3. Transfer **CROCK-POT**® stoneware insert from heating unit to heatproof surface. Allow bread pudding to cool and set before serving. Serve with berries and garnish with mint leaves, if desired.

Makes 10 to 12 servings

Pecan-Cinnamon Pudding Cake

1. Coat **CROCK-POT®** slow cooker with nonstick cooking spray or butter. Combine flour, granulated sugar, baking powder, and cinnamon in medium bowl. Add milk and 3 tablespoons butter; mix just until blended. Stir in pecans. Spread on bottom of **CROCK-POT®** slow cooker.

2. Combine water, brown sugar, and remaining 2 tablespoons butter in small saucepan; bring to a boil. Pour over batter in **CROCK-POT®** slow cooker. *Do not stir.*

3. Cover; cook on HIGH 1¼ to 1½ hours or until toothpick inserted into center comes out clean. Let stand, uncovered, for 30 minutes, then invert onto serving plate. Serve warm with whipped cream, if desired.

Makes 8 servings

1⅓ cups all-purpose flour
½ cup granulated sugar
1½ teaspoons baking powder
1½ teaspoons ground cinnamon
⅔ cup milk
5 tablespoons butter or margarine, melted, divided
1 cup chopped pecans
1½ cups water
¾ cup packed brown sugar
Whipped cream (optional)

Peach Cobbler

2 packages (16 ounces each) frozen peaches, thawed and drained

¾ cup plus 1 tablespoon sugar, divided

2 teaspoons ground cinnamon, divided

½ teaspoon ground nutmeg

¾ cup all-purpose flour

6 tablespoons butter, cut into small pieces

Whipped cream (optional)

1. Combine peaches, ¾ cup sugar, 1½ teaspoons cinnamon and nutmeg in medium bowl. Place into **CROCK-POT**® slow cooker.

2. For topping, combine flour, remaining 1 tablespoon sugar and remaining ½ teaspoon cinnamon in small bowl. Cut in butter with pastry blender or two knives until mixture resembles coarse crumbs. Sprinkle over peach mixture. Cover; cook on HIGH 2 hours.

3. Serve with freshly whipped cream, if desired.

Makes 4 to 6 servings

Spiced Plums and Pears

1. Cut pear slices in half with spoon. Place pears, plums, sugar, cinnamon, ginger and lemon peel in **CROCK-POT**® slow cooker. Cover; cook on HIGH 4 hours.

2. Combine cornstarch and water to make smooth paste. Stir into fruit mixture. Cook on HIGH until slightly thickened.

3. Serve warm or at room temperature over pound cake. Garnish with whipped topping, if desired.

Makes 6 to 8 servings

2 cans (29 ounces each) sliced pears in heavy syrup, undrained
2 pounds red or black plums (about 12 to 14), pitted and sliced
1 cup packed brown sugar
1 teaspoon ground cinnamon
½ teaspoon ground ginger
¼ teaspoon grated lemon peel
2 tablespoons cornstarch
2 tablespoons water
Pound cake or ice cream
Whipped topping (optional)

Bananas Foster

12 bananas, cut into
quarters
1 cup flaked coconut
1 teaspoon ground
cinnamon
½ teaspoon salt
1 cup dark corn syrup
⅔ cup butter, melted
2 teaspoons grated lemon
peel
¼ cup lemon juice
2 teaspoons rum
12 slices pound cake
1 quart vanilla ice cream

1. Combine bananas and coconut in **CROCK-POT**® slow cooker.

2. Stir together cinnamon, salt, corn syrup, butter, lemon peel, lemon juice and rum in medium bowl. Pour over bananas. Cover; cook on LOW 1 to 2 hours.

3. Arrange bananas on pound cake slices. Top with ice cream and warm sauce.

Makes 12 servings

Cherry Delight

1. Place pie filling in **CROCK-POT**® slow cooker.

2. Mix together cake mix and butter in medium bowl. Spread evenly over cherry filling. Sprinkle walnuts on top.

3. Cover; cook on LOW 3 to 4 hours or HIGH 1½ to 2 hours. Spoon into serving dishes, and serve warm with whipped topping or ice cream, if desired.

Makes 8 to 10 servings

1 can (21 ounces) cherry pie filling
1 package (18¼ ounces) yellow cake mix
½ cup (1 stick) butter, melted
⅓ cup chopped walnuts
Whipped topping or ice cream (optional)

1¾ cups packed light brown sugar, divided
2 cups all-purpose flour
¼ cup plus 3 tablespoons unsweetened cocoa powder, divided, plus additional for dusting, if desired
2 teaspoons baking powder
1 teaspoon salt
1 cup milk
4 tablespoons (½ stick) butter, melted
1 teaspoon vanilla
3½ cups boiling water

Hot Fudge Cake

1. Coat **CROCK-POT®** slow cooker with nonstick cooking spray or butter. Mix 1 cup sugar, flour, 3 tablespoons cocoa powder, baking powder, and salt in medium bowl. Stir in milk, butter and vanilla. Mix until well blended. Pour into **CROCK-POT®** slow cooker.

2. Blend remaining ¾ cup sugar and ¼ cup cocoa powder in small bowl. Sprinkle evenly over mixture in **CROCK-POT®** slow cooker. Pour in boiling water. *Do not stir.*

3. Cover; cook on HIGH 1¼ to 1½ hours or until cake tester inserted into center comes out clean. Allow cake to rest 10 minutes, then invert onto serving platter or scoop into serving dishes. Serve warm; dust with cocoa powder, if desired.

Makes 6 to 8 servings

Peanut Fudge Pudding Cake

1. Coat **CROCK-POT®** slow cooker with nonstick cooking spray or butter. Combine flour, ½ cup sugar and baking powder in medium bowl. Add milk, oil, vanilla and peanut butter. Mix until well-blended. Pour batter into **CROCK-POT®** slow cooker.

2. Combine remaining ½ cup sugar and cocoa powder in small bowl. Stir in water. Pour into **CROCK-POT®** slow cooker. *Do not stir.*

3. Cover; cook on HIGH 1¼ to 1½ hours or until toothpick inserted into center comes out clean. Allow cake to rest 10 minutes, then invert onto serving platter or scoop into serving dishes. Serve warm with chopped peanuts and ice cream, if desired.

Makes 4 servings

1 cup all-purpose flour
1 cup sugar, divided
1½ teaspoons baking powder
⅔ cup milk
2 tablespoons vegetable oil
1 teaspoon vanilla
½ cup peanut butter
¼ cup unsweetened cocoa powder
1 cup boiling water
Chopped peanuts (optional)
Vanilla ice cream (optional)

Index

Metric Conversion Chart

VOLUME MEASUREMENTS (dry)

$1/8$ teaspoon = 0.5 mL
$1/4$ teaspoon = 1 mL
$1/2$ teaspoon = 2 mL
$3/4$ teaspoon = 4 mL
1 teaspoon = 5 mL
1 tablespoon = 15 mL
2 tablespoons = 30 mL
$1/4$ cup = 60 mL
$1/3$ cup = 75 mL
$1/2$ cup = 125 mL
$2/3$ cup = 150 mL
$3/4$ cup = 175 mL
1 cup = 250 mL
2 cups = 1 pint = 500 mL
3 cups = 750 mL
4 cups = 1 quart = 1 L

VOLUME MEASUREMENTS (fluid)

1 fluid ounce (2 tablespoons) = 30 mL
4 fluid ounces ($1/2$ cup) = 125 mL
8 fluid ounces (1 cup) = 250 mL
12 fluid ounces ($1 1/2$ cups) = 375 mL
16 fluid ounces (2 cups) = 500 mL

WEIGHTS (mass)

$1/2$ ounce = 15 g
1 ounce = 30 g
3 ounces = 90 g
4 ounces = 120 g
8 ounces = 225 g
10 ounces = 285 g
12 ounces = 360 g
16 ounces = 1 pound = 450 g

DIMENSIONS

$1/16$ inch = 2 mm
$1/8$ inch = 3 mm
$1/4$ inch = 6 mm
$1/2$ inch = 1.5 cm
$3/4$ inch = 2 cm
1 inch = 2.5 cm

OVEN TEMPERATURES

250°F = 120°C
275°F = 140°C
300°F = 150°C
325°F = 160°C
350°F = 180°C
375°F = 190°C
400°F = 200°C
425°F = 220°C
450°F = 230°C

BAKING PAN SIZES

Utensil	Size in Inches/Quarts	Metric Volume	Size in Centimeters
Baking or Cake Pan (square or rectangular)	8×8×2	2 L	20×20×5
	9×9×2	2.5 L	23×23×5
	12×8×2	3 L	30×20×5
	13×9×2	3.5 L	33×23×5
Loaf Pan	8×4×3	1.5 L	20×10×7
	9×5×3	2 L	23×13×7
Round Layer Cake Pan	8×1½	1.2 L	20×4
	9×1½	1.5 L	23×4
Pie Plate	8×1¼	750 mL	20×3
	9×1¼	1 L	23×3
Baking Dish or Casserole	1 quart	1 L	—
	1½ quart	1.5 L	—
	2 quart	2 L	—